Lines for Living

Lines for Living

Mary Kennedy

HACHETTE
BOOKS
IRELAND

First published in 2011 by Hachette Books Ireland

1

A CIP catalogue record for this title is available from the British Library.

ISBN 978 1 444 72530 8

Typeset in Sabon MT and Roelandt BT
Printed in Great Britain by Clays Ltd, St Ives plc

Hachette Books Ireland policy is to use papers that are natural, renewable and recyclable products and made from wood grown in sustainable forests. The logging and manufacturing processes are expected to conform to the environmental regulations of the country of origin.

Hachette Books Ireland
8 Castlecourt Centre
Castleknock
Dublin 15, Ireland
A division of Hachette UK Ltd
338 Euston Road
London NW1 3BH

www.hachette.ie

For Eva, Tom, Eoin and Lucy.
Your presence in my life has opened my heart
in ways I could never have imagined possible.

The publisher would like to thank Random House Group Ltd for kind permission to reproduce quotations from *Benedictus: A Book of Blessings* by John O'Donohue, published by Bantam Press.

Contents

Starting Over

"Lift up your eyes upon
The day breaking for you.
Give birth again
To the dream."

Maya Angelou

And so in the middle of January 2011, I take up my position at the trusty computer to start work on another tome, to give birth again to the dream! A sequel to *Lines I Love*, which was published in 2007 and sold really well, was shortlisted for an Irish Book of the Year award in 2008, and which I remember writing with great affection. Admittedly, there were occasions during the process that were tiring and occasions when I would have preferred to wash the floors or clean the toilets rather than sit down at the computer and write another chapter but, overall, it was a pleasurable and satisfying experience and I am proud of the work I put into it and delighted by the response it has received (and still continues to receive) from the people who read it.

A number of people went to the trouble of writing to me after they'd read the book to say it had given them a bit of inspiration, a bit of encouragement, a bit of consolation or comfort. For some readers, it provided an accessible route to nostalgia and memories of their childhoods and growing up in a very different Ireland. I was thrilled to receive through the post quotations that had struck a chord with readers, quotations that they wanted me to have. One particular envelope included individual strips of paper with various quotations, carefully typed and accredited to their various authors. This took a lot of time and I am grateful for and humbled by the trouble the sender took in order for me to have those lovely lines. One of those quotations seems appropriate this minute. It's a piece of advice from none other than David Lloyd George:

"Don't be afraid to take big steps.
You can't cross a chasm in two small jumps."

David Lloyd George

Why do you think this particular sentence is hitting the spot for me right now rather than the beautiful uplifting and positive words of Maya Angelou at the beginning of the chapter? Because I'm scared! I need to be encouraged, motivated, pushed. I know I've got two books under my belt at this stage. As well as *Lines I Love*, I wrote a memoir called *Paper Tigers* in 2004. So I have a track record and I keep telling myself that but, still, the thought of embarking on another book is daunting. What if I have nothing to say? What if I can't meet the publisher's deadline? What if there aren't enough suitable quotations in my files to illustrate and enhance the text? What if I embark on this project and get cold feet halfway through? There is no shortage of 'what ifs'. As Joan of Arc said in George Bernard Shaw's play *Saint Joan*:

"If ifs and ands were pots and pans,
there'd be no need of tinkers."

St Joan of Arc

On the two previous occasions when I decided to step up to the plate and bare my soul and, more particularly, my heart, because I have always written what I truly felt and experienced, the 'what ifs' have not reared their ugly disconcerting heads. I was not bothered about what people might think of me. I didn't care if there were people out there whose response to my book arriving on the shelves was to mutter to themselves, 'And who does she think she is?' – I genuinely felt this way from the very beginning, not knowing that they were going to be well received. I was writing for myself and for the people who would pick it up, read it and be glad they had. If those people who would fall into the category of begrudgers did try to pop their heads above the parapet, I was able to push them back down again, reciting to myself one of my favourite quotations:

"People too weak to follow their own dreams will always find a way to discourage yours."

AMOS BRONSON ALCOTT

These wise words of Amos Bronson Alcott, an American teacher and philosopher who lived from 1799 to 1888, make him a man after my own heart in many ways. For instance, he felt that communication with his students would be enhanced using a conversational style, something that was unheard of at the time. I'm with him on that one. In fact, it's the only way I can write anything, so thank you Amos. He also advocated a vegan diet before the term existed, believing that abstinence and temperance led to physical well being that, in turn, improved mental performance. Although I can see where he might be coming from, I have to part company with him there. For me, all food is one of the great pleasures of life. In fact (note to self), I believe the celebration of food and wine and gathering together deserves a chapter in this book! Amos was also a staunch advocate and campaigner for women's rights and status, and he must have put his money where his mouth was because he had four daughters, one of whom went on to write one of the all-time classics of American literature, *Little Women*. Amos, not surprisingly given his liberal and pupil-centred thinking, wasn't the best at earning enough money to support his family and it was Louisa May who provided for them all following the success of her novels. I'm sure she did so willingly. Her father seems to have been a positive, loving force in her life and in the lives of many others, including mine, when I remember his lines about following your dreams.

Why, therefore, am I having doubts about embarking on this book? Why do I think it won't be as popular or as pleasing as the previous two? What's changed in three years? The truth is a lot has changed and, therefore, there is a good reason to take the bull by the horns and record some more moments that are meaningful and make up the rich tapestry of life, and to share some more of the quotations that gave me a lift when I discovered them. I can relate to the sentiments expressed and get consolation sometimes in the knowledge that other people encounter similar obstacles to myself.

A second truth is that in the past three years I have changed. I have lived through the transition from full-on mothering – I was a woman who was multitasking, juggling work, home, school runs, lunches, matches – to a woman whose children have become young adults, who have their own lives and who are happy and fulfilled doing their own thing. They don't want, or need, their dinner on the table at seven every evening. In a lot of ways, I'm redundant. I know that's the game plan from the time children are born, that they grow up, nurtured and loved and educated in the ways of the world and the people with whom they share it. They've put in years of listening to advice and hopefully some of it has been absorbed and played a part in the people they have become. Advice like that given by Jayne Jaudon Ferrer in her poem 'Essential Minutiae':

"Promptly send your thank-you notes.
Promptly pay your bills.

Promptly flush and wash your hands.
Promptly wipe up spills."

JAYNE JAUDON FERRER

ꝏ

They listen, they hear, they grow up, and they develop their own personalities and have their own lives. I wouldn't want it any other way but, my goodness, it takes some getting used to. We will talk about this phenomenon at length between the covers of this book.

Another change that has occurred in the past few years is, of course, the intermittent lapse in self-confidence which I was feeling deeply as I began to write this chapter but which I'm pleased to say is diminishing as I get further into the writing. I'm actually enjoying it now in a way that I didn't think was possible when I opened up the laptop. That's another thing that's changed, by the way. *Paper Tigers* and *Lines I Love* were both written on the big and bulky, but much loved and trusted, desktop computer. I invested in this laptop before Christmas because the old computer is upstairs in a darker room and, given my feelings of dark and foreboding as I prepared this project, I decided I needed to be in a light and airy room so I set up shop in the dining room looking out through the conservatory to the garden and, even in the depths of winter, my spirits will always be lifted by 'the wonder of a garden', as the late and great Irish poet and philosopher John O'Donohue refers to it in his poem 'In Praise of Earth'.

"The wonder of a garden
Trusting the first warmth of spring
Until its black infinity of cells
Becomes charged with dream."

JOHN O'DONOHUE

This is a positive, optimistic view of the garden, full of hope, looking forward to the moment when the garden brightens 'beneath a vision of colour'. I share that view of the garden and I am hoping that, by sitting here with a clear view of the outdoors, a positive and optimistic viewpoint will pervade my thinking and keep the lapses in confidence and the negative 'what ifs' at bay.

'In Praise of Earth' is published in John O'Donohue's book of blessings *Benedictus* which I was delighted to get as a Christmas present three years ago. That was December 2007. He died suddenly, at the age of fifty-one, in January 2008. Another startling reminder that it's important to live every moment to the full; to embrace, as he did, all the opportunities and challenges that life throws our way. Another reason to take this opportunity to gather together the lines that are meaningful to me and to share them, so that they may lighten the load, or shorten the road, for some reader.

The most significant change that's happened to me in the past few years is the endurance and survival of the menopause. Now this is a subject that deserves, and will be given, a chapter all to itself, the dear thing! I mention it here because it is no doubt responsible for the lapses in self-confidence and the negative and dark thoughts that worm their way into my consciousness from time to time. I am, by disposition, a person with a bright and positive outlook on life. I am gregarious by nature, but when the *M* monster decides to attack, all positive thinking fades and dissipates and is replaced by a cocktail of anxiety, panic and a lorry-load of 'what ifs'. During those moments, I have found it really helpful to have appropriate lines to hand. They might not lift my mood at the time, but they do remind me 'that this too will pass'! It's important to remember the words of the American novelist Madeleine L'Engle when you're feeling a bit vulnerable about the passing years:

"The great thing about getting older is that you don't lose all the other ages you've been."

MADELEINE L'ENGLE

ꝗ

L'Engle died in 2007, at the age of eighty-eight, having lived a varied and fulfilling life, which included doing badly at school, being told she was stupid, acting in New York, marrying an actor, having three children, renovating and running a grocery store with her husband, writing award-winning fiction (particularly for young adults), giving talks on her Christian beliefs and being honoured with many accolades. Quite a tally that for a woman who couldn't concentrate in school and proof that life is about the accumulation of the good and the bad things that happen to us, that blend together to make us what we are. I remind myself of this when the anxiety and panic lead me to lose faith in myself.

I know I'm not alone in this. I have heard similar stories from other women who are also at 'the middle day of human life', which is a lovely way of describing middle age, a stage in life that follows naturally from the heady days of childhood, adolescence, young adulthood and maturity. It is as inevitable and natural a fact of life, for both men and women, as is the fact that night follows day. There is no escape. The tone of that sentence though is gentle and accepting. It's from the pen of Jean Ingelow, a nineteenth-century English poet and novelist who was known for her gentle character and her sweetness of sentiment. When I think of middle age as 'the middle day of human life', I'm conscious of its value, its status in relation to other stages in life, the humanity, the wisdom, the acceptance that comes with living and with different experiences. All in all, middle age has a lot going for it. Women though, for the most part, have to be reminded of this because, of all the life stages, it is the one that brings with it profound feelings of loss of worth, loss of attraction and loss of control over our destiny. Those feelings of fragility are partly due to the physical and hormonal changes happening in our bodies. Thank you menopause! They are also partly due to the perception that youth and physical beauty are the yardsticks by which we should judge humanity. What an inadequate and shallow view of the world that is. We must rail against it at every opportunity and persist in the assertion that:

"First you are young; then you are middle-aged; then you are old; then you are wonderful."

LADY DIANA COOPER

❦

Those words were spoken by the English socialite and actress, Lady Diana Cooper, who was in her nineties when she died in 1986 and who, when she was young, was widely regarded as the most beautiful woman in England. Wise woman, Lady Diana!

With this affirmation ringing in my ears, and with the knowledge that there will be moments of self-doubt and fear, I will embark on this project and gather my thoughts and lines to share them and explain why they are central to my sense of well being, my treasured memories. I hope that they will have the same uplifting and comforting effect for those who read them. I will disregard the begrudgers, and I will take the advice of the late Nuala O'Faolain in *Best Love, Rosie*, the last book she wrote before she died.

❦

"Risk yourself still.
But remember, recovery time is shorter now
than it ever was. Respect the way things are.
Ground yourself not on what might have been,
but on what is."

NUALA O'FAOLAIN

Empty Nest

"Little children, headache;
big children, heartache."

ITALIAN PROVERB

ঙ

This Italian proverb sums up how I was feeling during the summer of 2010. My eldest child, Eva, decided to move out of home and into an apartment with a friend. This was a very strange experience for me and I found it hard to come to terms with the change. And yes, I did feel a lot of heartache and I missed her terribly. In the months preceding the move, I shared this catastrophic event with friends and colleagues during the course of many conversations and they were all very sympathetic and made soothing and comforting pronouncements about it being tough, but that it would become bearable and sure wasn't that the way of the world, and so on and so forth. Invariably, the question would be asked as to Eva's age at this pivotal stage in her and her mother's existence and when I proffered the information that she was twenty-six, they would all guffaw with peals of laughter, recounting their own experiences of coming up to Dublin from the country at the tender age of seventeen or eighteen, having to fend for themselves in cold and miserable bedsits in Rathmines or Drumcondra, and the way it toughened them up and made them wise in the ways of the world.

I believe all those stories. I know that when I left school and started in UCD, I was envious of the country students who had to live away from home and I would gladly have swapped my warm and comfortable home in Clondalkin for a damp bedsit in Rathmines or Ranelagh. Can you imagine the freedom and the parties! In those days of the seventies, though, it would have been frowned upon for somebody to leave home when it wasn't necessary. What would it say about your relationship with your parents? It would have been lovely to have the independence and freedom, but it just wasn't going to happen. I have to admit that this was one of the fears that ran through my mind as Eva was planning to move out. What would it say about our relationship? I didn't want people to think we didn't get on. I was afraid they'd think that there was a mother–daughter clash. Fear was very much part of the experience for me at the time. And one of the things I have come to know about fear – and had confirmed by Marilyn French, the American feminist, writer and novelist – is that:

"Fear is a question.
What are you afraid of and why?
Our fears are a treasure house of
self-knowledge if we explore them."

MARILYN FRENCH

A part of me was afraid of what people might think. I didn't want anyone to think Eva was moving out because we were rowing, or that I was controlling, or that she'd have more freedom in an apartment. For me, there are two elements of self-knowledge in the exploration of that fear. Firstly, it was pride that was making me worry about what people would or would not think. Why should I care what they think? The truth is I shouldn't care, but when we're feeling vulnerable, our self-esteem takes a knock and we do care. I know that's pride and I know that pride is a destructive and a dangerous sentiment. As Carl Jung says:

"Through pride we are ever deceiving ourselves.
But deep down below the surface of the average
conscience, a still, small voice says to us,
something is out of tune."

CARL JUNG

Something was certainly out of tune for me to have those concerns, but I have to add that it's only when we're feeling strong, confident and forthright that we listen to that 'still small voice' and we say, 'To hell with what people think!'

The second nugget of self-knowledge that I gleaned from the exploration of this fear is that things are very different nowadays from the time when it would have been frowned upon for somebody living in Dublin to move out into a 'bedsit', as they were called in those days. My children have more freedom to come and go as they please than was the norm in my day. I don't ask questions of them in the same way as parents quizzed their offspring in former times. I remember reading somewhere that you know your child is growing up and away from you when the incessant questions about where he came from are replaced with stony silence about where he's going!

Something that is universal though, and I have only fully appreciated since my daughter left home, is the heartache and loneliness that a child's move can trigger in a mother's heart. I remember vividly the day I finally left home and the lonely look on my mother's face. It was April 1982. I had just returned from honeymoon in Portugal and called to my mother's house to pick up some things to bring to the house that I would share with my new husband. It was a happy and exciting time for us, but it was tinged with sadness because I knew there was something wrong with my mother. She wasn't jumping for joy and sharing in the excitement of setting up this first home. In fact, as we were leaving and shouting our goodbyes to the assembled family, she didn't turn around from the kitchen sink. I couldn't understand why, and I have to admit I was a bit cross with her and felt she had been rude not to. It's true she had been widowed five years earlier at age fifty-eight and that I was the oldest of her four children. What's also true, but I didn't appreciate it at the time, is that her heart was probably breaking with a sense of loss and loneliness that another of her children was leaving home for good (my younger brother John had married two years before me).

For twenty-eight years, my mother had been mistress of a bustling, busy, often noisy house. Her family and her community in Clondalkin were of paramount importance to her. She was of the generation that had to leave her civil service job in the College of Science when she got married and she concentrated all her energy on home-making and raising her family. She would have agreed wholeheartedly with Stephen R. Covey, author of the bestselling and highly inspirational work, *The Seven Habits of Highly Effective People*, when he wrote the following about parenting:

ꝶ

"I think the most significant work
we ever do, in our whole world,
is done within the four walls of our own home."
Stephen R. Covey

ꝶ

My mother certainly did significant work within the four walls of our house in Clondalkin. She reared four children. I'm the oldest; my brother John is two years younger than me. Then there's my sister Deirdre and my younger brother Tony. We were all loved deeply and none of us was spoiled. My mother was great fun, but very strict and had a deep sense of duty and responsibility. I think I speak for the four of us when I say we were far more wary of crossing her than our father. I suppose by modern standards they had a good cop, bad cop vibe going on and we knew well that we could get away with things when Dad was in charge that you wouldn't dream of chancing if Mam was around.

I remember many occasions when we kids thought we were hard done by. Others on the road were allowed stay out later to play. We didn't like having to do chores like washing blackcurrants after a visit to the country or polishing silver before being allowed out at all during the summer holidays. I hated having to eat porridge for breakfast in the winter – I can't abide it to this day. I'm the same with prunes, which were visited on us once a week. We took piano lessons, were sent to elocution lessons, to Irish dancing and swimming classes, even though there was precious little money to spare.

We didn't always appreciate those extracurricular activities, and I certainly didn't appreciate having to spring clean the house and wash the windows during Holy Week in preparation for Easter, not to mention that we had a track worn to the church that same week to take part in all the ceremonies. My mother had a deep faith and ours was a traditional Irish Catholic family. We knelt down in the kitchen every evening after tea to say the Rosary, despite our best efforts to hide the rosary beads or make an excuse of some pressing homework that had to be done. If it had to be done, it would be done after 'the prayers', as my mother always referred to the Rosary. As I said, we four thought we had it tough but, looking back, I can appreciate that we were very lucky to have had such a grounded, simple, happy, no-nonsense upbringing. I reckon that's a view shared by many people my age when they look back and compare their lives then with modern living. I know it's the view of Seamus Hogan, a man who, after he read *Lines I Love,* sent me a letter and a poem that he had written himself, remembering his own childhood and his family's tradition of saying the Rosary. The poem is entitled 'Decade' and in it he refers to 'the prayers' and has memories of:

"Between the mysteries, the pinching,
the faces and the smirks."

SEAMUS HOGAN

I remember those moments very well myself. Trying not to laugh out loud while all around you are hell bent on getting you into trouble. The ending of Seamus' poem is quite poignant and indicative of that realisation that they were, indeed, happy days:

"Many's the time since then
I've prayed, without smiling,
For a heaven just like those nights
When the Rosary was said."

SEAMUS HOGAN

Those busy days of mothering and minding and rearing and scolding and laughing were undoubtedly very fulfilling for my mother, and their demise, as first my father died suddenly at the age of fifty-nine and then my brother and I left home to be married, must have made her very sad and very lonely. It's only now as I experience the beginnings of my children's leave taking that I properly understand that loneliness and emptiness and lack of purpose, and why my mother didn't turn around from the sink on that day in 1982.

Like my mother, I also have four children, two boys and two girls with similar age gaps as between myself and my brothers and sister. I'm divorced, therefore experiencing the leave taking alone, as did my mother. When the children were small, my life revolved around their routines, their schools, matches, piano, art, speech and drama. Doesn't that sound familiar! When you throw into the mix the fact that I have always worked outside the home, firstly as a teacher and then in RTÉ, I reckon I was just as busy as Mam was when I was a child. And I loved every minute of it. I was very lucky in that my mother was my childminder and she adored all her grandchildren and they did her. She was a typical granny, checking the homework, allowing the children to feed the birds, drawing houses, cats and boats, reading, telling stories and making sugar sandwiches for tea. As the saying goes:

ᘓ

“No cowgirl was ever faster on the draw than a grandma pulling baby pictures out of her handbag.”

ᘓ

My mother was very proud of all of her ten grandchildren and very happy to spend time with them. She was a wonderful support to me when my children were small and was always willing to help out when she could. They were busy days. Chances are there’s more than one small, adorable child in the family at any given time – I had four children under the age of seven at one point – and there are so many boxes to be ticked every single day for mothers, those who work inside and outside the home. I’ve often thought that it’s such a pity that when our children are small and adorable, we mothers are at our lowest ebb.

I spent hours every weekend making up baby dinners and liquidising them for the week ahead – fabulous, lip-smacking combinations like liver and potato, carrot and potato, lamb chop and broccoli, and chicken and celery (which needed extra sieving to remove the strings). The thinking behind those gourmet sessions was, of course, to get good, nourishing food into my babies and to educate their taste buds to enjoy wholesome food. Oh the naiveté of that! They've turned out to be good eaters and enjoy good food, but I don't delude myself – if they were to choose between liver and pizza or goujons on a menu, their months of eating those puréed delights would not influence their decision in any positive way. A bit like me with porridge and prunes I suppose.

School lunches were another hurdle to be scaled. What would they eat? What would the teacher allow? What would they swap as soon as my back was turned? What would keep them going so that they wouldn't arrive home like a bag of cats because they were hungry? There's a Japanese proverb which sums up this dilemma very neatly:

"In a child's lunchbox, a mother's thoughts."

JAPANESE PROVERB

Isn't it comforting to know that even on the other side of the world, in a culture totally different from ours, the important issues are the same! I remember so well those early-morning sessions of filling the lunchboxes. I remember the different colours and logos, from My Little

Pony and Thomas the Tank Engine to Transformers and Beauty and the Beast. I remember closing them and my thoughts would turn to the day ahead for my four children. I hoped they would be happy in school, part of the group, not under pressure, and have other children to play with in the yard. Then I would put the lunchboxes in the equally colourful, sometimes even matching, school bags and the fun would start. Missing tie, tracksuit day instead of uniform, no pencil – a lot of rushing and shouting and perspiration and a sigh of relief when I delivered them to the school and could go on to a civilised day with adults.

I wonder what their memories are of those days. Jayne Jaudon Ferrer writes of her childhood memories in a poem called 'Missing the Touch'.

"My best memory is of chilly winter mornings
when my mother draped my school clothes
over the furnace.
Warm from the fire,
warm from the heartflush of knowing
I was indisputably,
irrefutably
loved."

JAYNE JAUDON FERRER

❦

I hope that my children remember those school mornings for the love and concern I put into their lunchboxes along with the food, and not so much for the times when it was a battle to get them up and dressed, fed and delivered to school on time. There were other, less stressful and more enjoyable times of the day when the children were very young. I loved that moment when I picked them up from school and they would be bursting with excitement to present me with their picture or some other wonderful craft they had made that day. I still have a lot of them, especially the Christmas decorations they made and which I insist on displaying every year. I loved bath time and then snuggling up with them in their cosy beds for a bedtime story. Wouldn't it be lovely to bottle those moments and have them forever?

❦

"It's when he sings to me I ache for time to stop."

JAYNE JAUDON FERRER

❦

Time doesn't stop though. It marches on, and children grow into teenagers and then adults and each stage

has its challenges, and its highs and lows. I enjoy my children at this adult stage. We go to the theatre and the cinema together. We meet up for coffee if we're in town at the same time. We go shopping for things they need if they're going travelling during the summer.

We have a weekend away every year, just the five of us, and we have promised that we will try to continue that tradition, no matter what the future holds. So far we've had wonderful trips together, to New York, to Krakow, to London. We do the tourist things. Take a bus tour, see a show, go to a match, eat out. These memories are very special. We have good fun and good chats – some of the best of them are last thing at night or first thing in the morning, when we're just hanging out in the bedrooms.

They have their own lives though. And that's as it should be. I know they are branching out from the home and looking in other directions. The result of that is that I am very vigilant about enjoying the time that I do spend with them. If Tom, for instance, who like his mother is a great tea drinker, comes into the kitchen and asks me if I'd like a cuppa, I leave what I'm doing and sit at the table with him. Sometimes we talk, sometimes we laugh at the antics of the cats, sometimes he reads me snippets from the paper. The fact is though that we are together. I am present to him. How I wish I had done that more when they were small. There were too many times when I would prepare the food, put it on the table and while the children were happily eating, I would take the opportunity to get some other job done. What a mistake. If I had that time back, I would do things differently. I would sit and watch them eat and chat and laugh. Or I think I would. That's with the benefit of hindsight, of course, and with the benefit of not having other chores needing attention.

Maybe it's when we have grandchildren that we get the opportunity to relate fully in that way. And maybe that's the way we repay our children for the joy and the innocence that they brought into our lives when they were small. I came across an interesting book of interviews in which grandmothers talked about their relationships with their children and grandchildren, and one of them seemed to be making that point. The book is called *Grandmothers Talking to Nell Dunn*. The name Nell Dunn will be familiar to anyone who saw the film *Up the Junction*, based on her 1963 award-winning novel of the same name, which gave a moving account of life in the industrial slums around Battersea and Clapham Junction. One of the grandmothers, who was called Stella, spoke of the extraordinary feeling of absolute love she felt when she held her baby granddaughter against her:

"... the physical sensation of her body
and feeling totally free to love her completely,
no complications.
With my own children perhaps
it was more suffocating,
but this felt just a freedom to love."

STELLA

It's not hard for me to understand what Stella means by the word 'suffocating'. It's easy to be suffocated by the demands of each day's 'to do' list, particularly where there are several children to be cared for – washing, cleaning, ironing, gardening and, in many cases, a job outside the home as well. From where I'm standing at the moment, looking back on the beautiful, innocent days when my children were small, I realise that I was always on the go, busy and juggling lots of different tasks. If I had the time back again, I'd like to think I would do things differently. Like Nadine Stair, the woman from Louisville, Kentucky, who when asked, at the age of eighty-five, what she would do if she had her life to live over, said:

"I would ride on more merry-go-rounds,
I would pick more daisies."
NADINE STAIR

However, the chances are that I would be just as hassled and just as busy. What I know is that I insist now on taking the time and being present to my children when we are together. As Sr Stan says in her book of reflections, *Moments of Stillness*:

"In the here
in the now
an eternal moment
gifting us with insight."
SR STAN

She's right. When I am with one of my children and not thinking about, or doing, anything else, the time is sweet, unhurried, a lovely connection between the two of us. I do feel I gain an insight into the person that is my child and I'm grateful for that. I wish I could have experienced this feeling of being as one with them when my children were small. If they, in the future, become parents themselves, I will certainly encourage them to be less hurried with their youngsters and to enjoy those early years – they pass so quickly and they are to be treasured.

Children can be demanding and exhausting and try your patience, but they are innocent and delightful and should be cherished. In the words of the American poet laureate William Stafford:

"Kids dance before they learn there
is anything that isn't music."

WILLIAM STAFFORD

It's good to remember that, in the moments when children are jumping about and wrecking your head as well as your home. I dearly wish that I had been more conscious of that aspect of their little personalities when they were small and so, so charming. I did enjoy them and love them, but I suppose I took those qualities for granted. I am eternally grateful for those years, but I would love to relive them and be present to them 'in the here, in the now'.

My children are adults now and I understand the loneliness and longing that my mother must have felt when her children left home. My transition from full-on mothering has been gradual. Over the past couple of years, they've all finished school. There are no deadlines to meet there any more, no school runs, not to mention the school lunches, uniforms and books. They have chosen their own leisure-time activities, everything from DIY to drama, to camogie, to running. They get themselves to these activities. When we have dinner together, it's pre-arranged and I enjoy cooking that family meal immensely. I make a special effort, cook what they like to eat and I look forward to us all being around the table together. But they have their own lives. I accept that and want them to be fulfilled and happy. In the words of John O'Donohue:

"May you feel life as an irresistible invitation
To discover and develop your talents,
Each day bringing something new to birth."

JOHN O'DONOHUE

ↄ

Those words hit the spot for me. That's exactly what I want for my children. That's what I reared them for – to look on life as full of opportunity and to make the most of what comes their way and suits their personalities and their talents. I want them to look upwards and outwards, rather than backwards or at me. I want them to go forward from the nest and fly. I think often of Liam O'Flaherty's short story, *His First Flight*, about the young seagull who was afraid to leave the nest, even though his siblings had already made the leap.

ↄ

"The young seagull was alone on his ledge.
His two brothers and his sister had already
flown away the day before.
He had been afraid to fly with them."

LIAM O'FLAHERTY

ↄ

I studied that story in my first year at secondary school and that wasn't today nor yesterday, and yet I remember it vividly. I can visualise the young bird, afraid to leave the security of the nest. The others have flown away to independence and the joys of catching their own fish and swimming and cavorting in the sea. His mother and father encourage him to fly away.

ᘓ

"... scolding him, threatening to let him starve on his ledge unless he flew away."

LIAM O'FLAHERTY

ᘓ

I think you'd describe that as 'tough love'! You'll be glad to know, therefore, that the story has a happy ending. Our hero finally plucks up the courage, takes his first flight and can't understand what he was afraid of. He relishes the freedom and the independence. The way of the world for birds and also for children. They should leave the nest. They do leave the nest. Unlike Mother Seagull, though, this mother feels the loss and sadness as this is happening, and it reached a level of intensity, as I said at the beginning of the chapter, when Eva moved into an apartment last year.

The move had been planned a year in advance, so it didn't come as a surprise. One of her friends, Anna, a young doctor, was going to work in New Zealand for a year and they agreed that they would share an apartment on her return. What do you do when you have a year to prepare for something? Nothing! I put it to the back of my mind and pressed on regardless. That brought me to summer, Anna's return after a wonderful year and 'The Move'. I dreaded it. I felt life would be very different with Eva gone. We were always very close and did a lot of things together. We had a TV date for *Grey's Anatomy* and *Desperate Housewives* on Tuesdays. We'd get into the jammies and make a pot of tea and eat tuna in pitta bread. And there were so many other things we did together that I knew I would miss. I was also afraid her relationship with her brothers and sister would diminish.

Needless to say, I didn't let Eva see this sadness and I helped her move her things with enthusiasm. And yes, it was very lonely and very strange in the beginning. Her room was empty and quiet. I realised I had to shop differently with one less person in the house. I wasn't looking forward to the return of *Grey's* or *Housewives*. Guess what though … I'm over it! It's been a great move for Eva. She's an independent young woman, who has to budget in a way that wouldn't be the case at home. She has a nice lifestyle, a comfortable apartment and a good friend and flatmate to have long, girly chats with. And she and I still see lots of each other. We still watch our programmes together, just a day later. Her room is no longer empty. It's amazing how you can fill empty presses and wardrobes. I wonder where I used to keep everything before! The apartment is lovely and cosy with stunning views over the Liffey. Herself and Anna would keep a candle factory in business. Eva and I still have all the old conversations and new ones as well, about recipes and what to cook for friends coming for dinner, about hanging baskets and balcony troughs and what to grow at different times of the year. The apple doesn't fall far from the tree!

When I reflect on all those twenty-seven years of child rearing, with its headaches and its heartaches, I realise that I am very proud of the adults my children have become. I love them as deeply now as when they were tiny, dependent little things, when they were boisterous, noisy, growing things, when they were questioning, adolescent things, when they are now adult, independent things. I want them to know that as they move onwards and upwards and into their own lives, there will always be an open door to my heart and to this house, calmer and quieter perhaps now, but still home.

"Someplace where there isn't any trouble,
someplace where your heart is nourished,
someplace where your soul is fed.
someplace that feels like Home."

JAYNE JAUDON FERRER

There but for the Grace of God

"Come away, O human child!
To the waters and the wild
With a faery, hand in hand,
For the world's more full of weeping
than you can understand."

W. B. YEATS

On a Sunday afternoon during the past winter, I went for a walk in the park with my two daughters. We came across a fairy tree which was obviously a well-known point of interest to some people, given the number of bits and pieces that were attached to it. The lines above, for instance, from Yeats' beautiful poem 'The Stolen Child' had been printed out, laminated and three or four copies tacked to the tree in various places. Even if they hadn't been, you'd be in no doubt that this is a fairy tree. On the very top, about fifteen feet from the ground, the tree has a platform on which has been built a very pretty fairy castle. It's got three turrets of the type you'd imagine Rapunzel leaned from in response to the request from the ground.

ᴓ

"Rapunzel, Rapunzel, let down your hair."

THE BROTHERS GRIMM

ᴓ

Any child who might harbour a suspicion that grown-ups were just pretending this was a fairy tree would have every ounce of doubt erased on looking skywards and seeing the tiny fairy castle, fashioned from potter's clay at the top. And they could also look at the pictures of fairies that other children have pinned to the tree, some of them of Tinkerbell, cut out of books and coloured in, others drawn freehand and some of them accompanied by a little note to the fairies telling them about Christmases or birthdays or other special occasions. There were trinkets too, like hair bobbins and ribbons and coins pushed into little hollows. And there was one very special package left at the foot of the tree. There was no accompanying note but I can just imagine the sacrifice and longing that accompanied the placing of the package. It was a plastic bag, tightly fastened at the top and in it were four soothers, all different, all well used. I thought of the child who woke up one morning and decided, or maybe was persuaded by a grown-up, that it was a good idea to gather up all the soothers and leave them at the foot of the fairy tree so that maybe some little baby who needed a soother could have one. I thought of the child moving towards the spot, depositing that treasure and wondered what thoughts were going through that little head as he or she moved away from the tree a big boy or girl who wouldn't be needing a soother any more.

It reminded me of when Lucy, who is now nineteen and with me on the walk, decided or, rather, agreed, that she wouldn't be needing her soother any more. She was the only one of my four children who used one. The other three had different comforters. She is the youngest and I reckon the fight was gone out of me by the time she arrived and I was happy to give her whatever she needed to keep her quiet. Within reason, of course. I would have drawn the line at certain additions to her bottle, which, so I have been told by people who tried them, worked well. I don't doubt for a minute that they did, but there are limits!

Anyway, Lucy got very fond of her soothers and kept a few spares with her always, just in case. She was known to loop them around her fingers like dress rings. In fact, I've seen some huge rings from accessory shops in the intervening years and Lucy's soothers would have given them a run for their money in the style stakes! Attached as she was to her soothers, the day finally did dawn when Lucy decided she was a big girl now and didn't need them any more. This moment of truth happened to coincide with our return trip from our summer holidays in Rosslare in County Wexford when, quite unexpectedly and without warning, Lucy opened the back window of the car and threw her two soothers out the window. May I apologise in retrospect for my daughter's moment of anti-social behaviour and act of littering. I must admit, though, that on the day, when I had recovered from the shock of seeing this little one in the rear-view mirror launching plastic missiles out the window, I was delighted to see the end of the blessed things. Lucy never looked back, either literally or metaphorically! I know it's a pivotal moment in a child's life and I did wonder how the little one who left the bag of soothers coped following this brave deed. I hoped there were no regrets that night at bedtime. As the author and historian Charlotte Gray says:

"Becoming a mother makes you a mother of all children. From now on, each wounded, abandoned, frightened child is yours.

You live in the suffering mothers of every race
and creed and weep with them.
You long to comfort all who are desolate."

CHARLOTTE GREY

ॐ

I agree wholeheartedly with that statement. Since the birth of my first child, I have related in a totally different way to stories concerning children. I became aware of this phenomenon very early into motherhood because Eva was a tiny baby when the Ethiopian famine of 1984 finally made it onto our television screens, thanks to BBC reporter Michael Buerk. I reacted to seeing those sad images of starving children in a totally different way to previous occasions. I had, of course, been saddened and shocked by pictures of hungry children from Biafra, for instance, years earlier, but this was different. Every time I saw a report from Ethiopia, it was Eva I could see on that television screen and my reaction was one of utter sadness and heartache, which surprised me with its intensity and was probably the driving force behind my becoming involved in African charities when my children were older. Definitely, when you have a child, you become, in a strange way, a mother to all children.

During our walk in the park, and following the innocent and moving recollections that accompanied the sight of the bag of soothers, came a very sad and sobering moment as I continued my examination of the bits and pieces around the fairy tree. I came upon a letter, written in a child's hand and pushed into a Polly Pocket folder to keep it dry. It was a letter which began 'Dear fairy' and included a list of thank yous to the fairy and a list of wishes. That all sounds rather sweet and appropriate for inclusion in a letter from a child to a fairy, but the nature of the wishes and the reasons for being grateful would make you want to find the letter writer and give him or her a big hug. I suppose it's more likely to have been a little girl writing a letter to a fairy, but who's to say? Desperate situations call for desperate measures and this child's apparent situation would melt a stone. The pieces below are as they were written, spellings and all.

ᘓ

"I wish the kids more friendly to me
and my brother and my mum."

"Can you help little brother do better in schwole.
I wish my brother dose not be picked out
on the road and in schwole."

ᘓ

You certainly would like to give that little one a hug, although, on second thought, forget hugs. No child should have to worry about things like that. It seems as if it's a case for Social Services intervention. That's not going to happen, though, because there is no way of finding out who wrote the letter. There's no photo, no signature, just another few examples of a child with a heavy burden who took the trouble to share her concerns with a fairy.

"I wish my da would visit us more."

"I hope my nanny's back will be better.
I wish I can have a better life.
I want my ma to have witherglze."

The last line had me perplexed and it took a while to work out that the wish was for the mother to have 'Weatherglaze'. What does that tell us about the living conditions of this child and her family? Damp and draughty are the words that spring to mind. And in case we were in any doubt, there's another request to the fairy.

"Will you help my Ma win the Lotto."

There is one positive chord struck in the letter:

"I loved the Christmas dinner in my nannys."

It was a Sunday afternoon in late January that my daughters and I took the dog for a walk in the park, so the Christmas dinner at nanny's house was still a nice memory for that child. Thank goodness for that. It should, of course, have been just one of many happy memories but somehow I have the impression that there weren't too many happy moments in the letter writer's life. In fact, the lines from Yeats' masterpiece, 'The Stolen Child', seemed all the more poignant and relevant in the case of this little person who had written this letter and pinned it to the fairy tree because, in the case of this child, there's no doubt that 'the world's more full of weeping than you can understand'.

I was very upset by reading that letter and couldn't get it out of my mind. I took a photo of it on my phone so that I'd remember it. I'm glad to say that my grown-up daughters were also saddened, but, for me, it was another of those Charlotte Gray moments, where '*each wounded, abandoned child is yours*'. My heart went out to that little human being whom I have never met, never will meet and yet I find myself hoping she's okay – not cold, not bullied, not worried all the time about her mother, her little brother, her nanny's back and wishing her da would visit. She also mentions an uncle and some cousins that she'd love to see as well. Heart-breaking stuff on a tree in Marlay Park in Dublin.

❧

"Children, ay forsooth,
They bring their own love with them
when they come."

JEAN INGELOW

❧

Jean Ingelow got it right with that maxim. I believe that every child comes into the world as a bundle of love and, in most cases, that love is reciprocated and parents put their energies into creating a good, healthy, satisfying life for their child, where comfort and love are the norm. It doesn't always happen though, and, my goodness, the letter on the fairy tree is just one tiny reminder of the fact that for so many children life is harder than it should be. It would break my heart to be the mother of that child who felt the need to write a letter to a fairy, that child who, as Jean Ingelow pointed out, brought her own love with her when she came. Unfortunately, life hasn't quite measured up for that little one the bundle of love that she brought didn't bring with it any guarantees of a life of comfort and security.

The sad thing is that this is the reality for so many children in this country of ours. We live in a very unequal society where, according to research carried out at the beginning of the year by Social Justice Ireland and Fr Sean Healy, a champion of the poor in this country, the top 10 per cent of households receive nearly 25 per cent of disposable income as opposed to the bottom 10 per cent who receive between 2 and 3 per cent. How can that be fair or just? It's not fair and it's an uphill struggle for the people in the lower echelons of society to pay bills, to buy clothes and food, and to look after their children. It's particularly tough these days where unemployment figures are so high – and are climbing all the time – but the greater injustice is that it was also tough for some people during the boom years because the reality is that:

ꝏ

"The rich are richer, and the poor are poorer ... and, as a rule, the greater are the riches of the rich and the poverty of the poor."

JOSIAH STRONG

ꝏ

Those are the words of Josiah Strong, a Protestant clergyman from Illinois who was well known as a religious and social commentator, espousing Christian socialism in the late nineteenth and early twentieth centuries. The man died in 1916 and the sorry fact is that although the Western world has known untold wealth since then, nothing changed for the poor. In fact, a modern take on Stone's words are those of US congressman, Dennis Kucinich. His name might ring a bell because he was a candidate for the Democratic nomination for president in 2004 and 2008. He voted against invading Iraq and there's an interesting anti-invasion metaphor in what he has to say about poverty.

ꝏ

"We have weapons of mass destruction we have to address here at home.

Poverty is a weapon of mass destruction.
Homelessness is a weapon of mass destruction.
Unemployment is a weapon of mass destruction."

DENNIS KUCINICH

And that three-pronged weapon of poverty, homelessness and unemployment certainly is a weapon of destruction. It destroys lives – individual life, family life, community life. You don't need to be a rocket scientist to work that out. Mahatma Gandhi, one of the greatest advocates of justice and peace who ever lived, referred to poverty as *'the worst form of violence'*. Gandhi was assassinated in 1948 but, way before that, the terminology associated with poverty was equally telling. Aristotle, the Greek philosopher who died in 322 BC, was of the opinion that 'the mother of revolution and crime is poverty'.

From the beginning of time, therefore, the vocabulary associated with poverty is that of revolution, crime, violence and mass destruction. Surprise, surprise! Shame on us then that we haven't taken responsibility and worked as a country with a conscience and a sense of responsibility to divide the purse more equally. We rely very heavily on the conscience and commitment of people like Sean Healy who devote their lives to improving the lot of the vulnerable in our society. To be more conscious of the need for social justice would be in our own interests, actually, given the fact that poverty can lead to crime and violence and there's been an increase in the number of house break-ins and thefts in these recent recessionary times. When we hear about another burglary or another theft, we thank our lucky stars it wasn't our house. When we hear of another gangland incident, we're happy that they're just fighting among themselves. We sit back and are glad that it doesn't affect us. It does affect us, though. It affected me recently in a way that I wasn't expecting.

I was sitting in the garda station waiting to have a form signed and couldn't help overhearing a conversation between two men. I say I couldn't help overhearing them, but they weren't trying to be discreet. They were loud and gruff and rough. The *f*-word served as adjective and adverb to describe everything they said. I learned from listening to them that they were both there to sign on because they were out on bail. One was a seasoned campaigner, had done this many times before and when the desk sergeant appeared was able to tell her which book and which line he should sign, Book 32, Line 33. Job done. He could go home. The younger lad was new to this exercise and could remember the number of the book but not the line he should sign. When he was told he'd have to come back with the number, the situation became heated and quite volatile and nasty. The sergeant showed remarkable restraint but was not for turning, despite an offer from the guy that he could sign a piece of paper and she could stick it in the book when he phoned in the number. The young lad showed no restraint, shouted and ranted and finally left, chastened and probably cognisant of the fact that he was risking a breach of his conditions of bail and where that might lead him. When they had both left, I was relieved. I was glad this incident had happened in the relative security of a garda station rather than in a takeaway, for example, where an altercation between the young man and the person on the other side of the counter might have had a very different outcome.

Later, in the comfort of my own home and having told the story to my family, my thoughts turned to those lines from Jean Ingelow about babies bringing their own love into the world when they are born. That love had certainly been knocked out of those two young men. What they had in common with each other was their criminal background, their disdain for authority, their poverty. They were both pale, skinny and cheaply dressed. I would hate to be on the receiving end of their criminality – but they weren't born criminals, burglars, thieves. They were blank canvases when they were born.

I wonder about their parents. Are they devastated by their sons' behaviour? Or not? I find it very sad to read court reports of distraught parents of young offenders, pleading on behalf of their children, or pleading for their children to be taken from them into a correction unit. Either scenario is devastating. John O'Donohue has a lovely blessing 'for the parents of one who has committed a crime'. It begins with an indication of how others will look on this person:

❧

"No one else can see beauty
In his darkened life now.
... He has become the mirror
Of the damage he has done."

John O'Donohue

❧

For the parent, though, there is another way of looking at him because:

❧

"He is yours in a way
No words could ever tell;

And you can see through
The stranger this deed has made him
And still find the countenance of your son."

JOHN O'DONOHUE

ᘛ

I hope that's the case for the two young men I came across in that Dublin garda station. I hope their parents care about them and can look beyond the damage their sons have done. The young men may never change. They may never mend their ways. They may go on to commit horrible crimes, but there has to be a place in our hearts that opens to the difficulties of such people and realises that 'there but for the grace of God go I', or somebody belonging to me. Like I said, they weren't born criminals. They were born babies, full of hope and possibility and, let's face it, if they had been born into an affluent family, they wouldn't be signing the book in a garda station. As members of a civilised society, we must learn to hate the sin but not the sinner.

Anyone who has read my previous book *Lines I Love* will be familiar with the fact that my mother had a hardback copybook in which, as a young woman, she collected quotations, thoughts and prayers. There's a paragraph she chose to include that is particularly relevant to the way we view people who break the law. It's attributed to Stopford Augustus Brooke, a churchman and writer who is well remembered for his writings on English literature. He was born in Letterkenny in County Donegal, the son of a clergyman. He was educated at Trinity College, Dublin, and was himself ordained into the Church of England in 1857, following which, he served as chaplain to a German empress, Empress Frederick and to Queen Victoria in 1872. Eight years later, Brooke left the Church of England because he could no longer accept its leading dogmas. He worked as a Unitarian minister and his sermons and teachings were well received. Brooke was also very highly regarded for his writings, particularly his anthologies of poetry and prose. William Butler Yeats said of him that: 'the reader who would begin a serious study of modern Irish literature should do so with Mr Stopford Brooke (and Mr Rolleston's) exhaustive anthology'.

It would seem that Stopford Brooke was a man of great conviction, whether he was concerned with literary matters or with humanity, because the piece my mother transcribed, in black ink, into her copybook shows him to have been a man with firm opinions about the way we view and the way we judge others:

'There is nothing that needs so much patience as just judgement of a man, or even of one act of a man. We ought to know his education, the circumstances of his life, the friends he has made or lost, his temperament, his daily work, the motives which filled the act, the health he had at the time, the books he was reading, the temptations of his youth – we ought to have the knowledge of God to judge him justly, and God is the only judge of a man.'

STOPFORD BROOKE

I accept that Stopford was of his time. He died in 1916 and there are now, as there were then, rights and wrongs to be addressed and courts of law to address them, but it's no harm, I believe, to remember the humanity of the person before the courts and the many and varied elements that go to make up a life. I believe in justice being done and being seen to be done, but I also believe strongly in compassion and in the respectful treatment of all people, including criminals.

Sr Helen Prejean will be well known to anyone who has seen the movie *Dead Man Walking*, starring Sean Penn and Susan Sarandon, who plays the part of Sr Helen. The film is based on the book she wrote describing her experiences as spiritual advisor to inmates on death row. Sr Helen is an advocate for the abolition of the death penalty because she believes that: 'no matter what they have done, people are worth more than the worst act of their life'.

I think of those two young men signing on in the garda station and I wonder if they have gone on to bigger crimes. They probably have or will do in the future. It's a shame and a pity and an indictment of our social responsibility that this is the probable scenario. Fr Peter McVerry has often decried this state of affairs, during the many years he has spent working first with homeless boys and now with homeless young people in Dublin. He's a Jesuit priest who opened his first hostel in a three-bedroomed flat in Ballymun in 1979, catering for homeless boys between the ages of twelve and sixteen. Today, the Peter McVerry Trust also runs a number of other facilities for young people, including drug services, supported accommodation and independent living, all with the focus on the people that society would rather forget – the homeless, the vulnerable. It's interesting that the philosophy of the Jesuit order is: 'Give me the boy and I'll show you the man.'

There is no doubt that the order turns out very fine young men from their schools in Ireland, schools like Belvedere, Clongowes, Gonzaga and Crescent. Young men who are well educated, polite, generous, caring and have a sense of social justice. Fr McVerry, as a Jesuit, subscribes to his order's adage and has seen it borne out in very different circumstances. I remember him pointing out a young boy to me in the inner city. The boy was about eight, playing on waste ground in a boisterous and carefree way with his pals. Peter McVerry knew the boy's circumstances and told me in no uncertain terms of his utter conviction that he would be in and out of trouble, in and out of jail, by the time he reached adulthood. 'Give me the boy and I'll show you the man.'

Three chilling illustrations there of the vulnerability of young people: the dismal prospects for an eight-year-old playing in Dublin's inner city, the rage and offensive behaviour of two young men in a garda station, and a letter written by a child to a fairy, hoping for things that were most unlikely to materialise. Reminders, I suppose, that for some young people, the world is certainly 'more full of weeping' than they can understand. Reminders also, I hope, that we are inclined to take our children's well being for granted sometimes. We shouldn't. We should be very grateful that we are lucky enough to be able to provide for our children, to feed and clothe them, to keep them warm, to send them to school and give them other activities that will enhance their lives. We must not underestimate the privilege of being the parent of children who are, for the most part, happy little human beings.

We should count our blessings and enjoy our children. I know I, for one, worried far too much when they were small. And when I think of the situations I have described here, my worries were silly, downright ridiculous, even.

I remember years ago, when my first child had just started primary school, driving to the school yard when I knew her class would be on their play time and just sitting watching to see that she was part of the group and that they were all playing happily. On one occasion, when I had taken up my discreet position in the car park which served both the school and the church, thus providing me with a bit of cover, I saw her on her own, walking up and down, while the others were playing in groups and laughing and shouting and chasing each other around the place. My heart nearly broke with the thought that she was out of the loop perhaps, ostracised. I wanted to go over straight away and find out if there was anything wrong. I didn't go, which is just as well. I don't think she'd have forgiven me yet, some twenty years later. I didn't rest easy though until I got her home from school that day and was reassured that she was perfectly happy and there was no issue whatsoever. She couldn't even remember whether she had played with people or was just 'relaxing' at play time!

I know worry is futile because, for the most part, what we worry about is never as bad as we anticipate. There's a Swedish proverb which underlines this:

"Worry often gives a small thing a great shadow."

SWEDISH PROVERB

And there is no point anyway in worrying about something over which we have no control or power. However, I don't think I'm alone in worrying constantly about my children, no matter what age they are! As the saying goes:

"A mother's worry never ends,
It evolves and grows and starts again."

We should be always thankful that we can provide for our children and that they're happy and healthy. They deserve the best we can give them and that differs according to people's circumstances. I know that I was able to provide a lot more for my children than my parents could. That's not the point though. Children know when they are loved and cared for. It is an accident

of birth where we are born and into which circumstances. Some of the happiest children I have ever encountered fall into the category described by Mother Teresa as 'the poorest of the poor'. Some of the unhappiest children I have encountered want for nothing in a material sense but something is lacking, and it's usually love.

I'm very grateful that my four children have grown into adults who love life, know how to enjoy themselves but seem to have an ability to care about how others are coping in this world. The two girls have travelled on charity trips to various places in Africa and Lucy has been to Calcutta with the Hope Foundation. That was a school trip during Transition Year which involved working in homes for street children. It was undoubtedly an eye-opening experience for a seventeen-year-old and on the night Lucy arrived home, I went into her room to find her lying on her bed with tears flowing down her cheeks. She told me she was sad looking around her room and realising how good her life was compared to the children she'd left behind in Calcutta. I was sorry to see her upset but I was glad that the experience had opened her eyes and her heart to the plight of those less fortunate, because in the words of Maya Angelou:

"If you find it in your heart to care for somebody else, you will have succeeded."

MAYA ANGELOU

❧

You don't have to travel to Calcutta or Africa to see young people whose lives are difficult and harsh. The scenarios depicted in these pages are very much home grown. They are of Dublin, but I've no doubt they are to be found replicated in many other parts of this country. We should take a bit more time and pay a bit more attention to the children who write letters to fairies and the eight-year-olds playing on waste ground, so that they don't end up ten years hence walking into garda stations calling for Book 32 and signing their name on Line 33.

To finish with the words of Harriet Beecher Stowe, the nineteenth-century American author of *Uncle Tom's Cabin* and champion of the cause of the negro slave:

❧

"It's a matter of taking the side of
the weak against the strong,
something the best people have always done."

HARRIET BEECHER STOWE

Bien dans sa Peau

"When grace is joined with wrinkles, it is adorable. There is an unspeakable dawn in happy old age."
VICTOR HUGO

I would never dream of writing anything about age or ageing without keeping in my mind's eye those two short sentences from the eighteenth-century French poet and novelist Victor Hugo. They are the essence of my attitude to the passage of time and, in my opinion, should be part of the curriculum for every child, boy and girl, the length and breadth of the country, so that they grow up realising the beauty and dignity of old age.

Every age and stage in life has its own particular beauty and worth but it's a sad fact that we are not as positive and appreciative of the later stages as we are of the early and youthful ones. This is not true of every culture. In China and India, for instance, older people are revered and cherished, and, on my travels in Africa, I have seen the respect that is afforded the elders in tribal villages. The elders are invariably men and they make the decisions for the community but, within the household, the matriarch in the form of the granny rules the roost. Sadly, in many circumstances, it's also the grandmother who is rearing the children because so many young parents have died of HIV/AIDS. If people from these ancient civilisations and cultures have such deep and genuine regard for older people, why is it not the same in this part of the world? Could it be that older people are not as good looking or as well groomed as younger people, or as they were themselves in their younger days? I know I could ask this question till I'm blue in the face and nobody would ever admit that that is a part of the truth in the 'civilised, sophisticated' world. No matter what kind of a gloss people try to put on the way we treat older human beings in our midst, that stage in life is not valued in the same way as other stages. And isn't that a shame, not to mention disrespectful.

The way I look at life, we are constantly evolving from the time we come into the world, learn to walk and talk, grow into childhood, adolescence, adulthood, maturity, middle age and beyond. The wonderful aspect of life is that we accumulate different experiences, skills, emotions and sensations as we live our lives and they just add to our tapestry and make it, not older and less valuable, but richer. As the American poet Emily Dickinson said of the passing years:

"We grow not older with years but
Newer every day."

EMILY DICKINSON

Isn't it nice to think of getting 'newer' every day, adding to what has gone before and celebrating and enjoying the grace of Hugo's 'unspeakable dawn'.

It's such a loss to disregard any stage of life and, unfortunately, here in the Western world, there is an inordinate emphasis on youth and beauty that leads to a lot of pressure, particularly on women, to hang on for dear life to one particular stage in life. The fact that this pressure coincides with the stage in life where women are likely to be juggling career and motherhood as well as trying to stay slim and sexy doesn't make it any easier. This is a very stressful and exhausting time for women and as the American feminist Gloria Steinem said:

"I have yet to hear a man ask for advice on how to combine a marriage and a career."

GLORIA STEINEM

I know that men have their concerns at different stages of life, which can also be overwhelming and very difficult to deal with, but I do think women have quite intricate and multi-layered existences that are different to men's and which are worth taking a look at. As Joan Borysenko wrote of women's lives in her book *A Woman's Journey to God*:

"The life process of women is more chaotic and disorderly, more circular and intuitive. Sometimes we can't see the next horizon until we step out of the old life."

JOAN BORYSENKO

I know exactly what she means, because I'm a woman and I have gone through many chaotic and disorderly stages in life. Juggling motherhood and work – with all its attendant feelings of guilt and responsibility – is right up there, but that's not the only stage of a woman's life that can be difficult. I speak from experience, having gone through a lot of them, and I have arrived now at middle age. If anybody had told me twelve months ago that I would sit willingly at the computer and write about women 'd'un certain age', as the French so delicately put it – middle-aged women to you and me – I would have opened a book in Paddy Power's and placed a sizeable bet that hell would freeze over before that would happen. Why is this? Why is there still a taboo of sorts about middle age and menopause for women? Why would I avoid writing about middle age, whereas I would have no problem writing about my childrearing years or my teenage years? The answer is that there is a perception abroad that middle age is the end of the good times for women. I'm pleased to say that this viewpoint is generally held by people who have yet to reach this pivotal point in their existence. All women who have reached the middle stage of life, and who have come to terms with the monumental changes it brings, can console themselves with the knowledge that every single one of those people who have this perception will be joining the middle-aged club at some stage.

Middle age is definitely a transitional period in a woman's life and it happens to us all, except, of course, and very sadly, the women who die prematurely. To quote John Mortimer:

"Growing older is a privilege denied to many."

JOHN MORTIMER

When I read that line I always think of Princess Diana, a woman who was at the prime of her beauty when she died in 1997, at the age of thirty-six. I wonder how she would have aged had she lived. She'd be fifty this year, middle aged, probably enduring the menopause, with all its annoying and unpleasant elements, but alive and delighted to be sharing in the joy of her elder son's marriage.

There's no doubt that middle age and the menopause are challenges to most women, but the stages that precede it are not always a bed of roses either. When I think back to how I felt at the different stages of my life, I'm reminded of certain hurdles that had to be jumped along the way. When I started school, I was the tallest in my class of girls and boys. My cousin William and I are the same age and we made our First Communion together and I am a good head and shoulders above him in the photographs. Not any more, thankfully. I stopped growing and he passed me out. I hated being tall then and I must have taken steps to rectify the situation by stooping while I walked because my mother was always telling me to 'straighten your shoulders' and threatening to bring me to a specialist who would give me a set of braces to keep my back straight and me standing to my full height. The thought of being lumbered with that fashion accessory did encourage me to walk tall, at least when I was approaching the house and my mother could see me.

You'd be forgiven for thinking that once the height issue had been straightened out (pardon the pun) and others had caught up with me, life would have been full of fun. I was, after all, part of a loving and attentive family, with an aunt and uncle and three cousins next door. There were great and happy times and I've documented them with affection and the joy of memories in *Lines I Love* but here as I concentrate on the vicissitudes of being a woman I'm remembering the difficult times.

"It's difficult to decide whether growing pains are something teenagers have or are."

I'm sure I had my moments, like all teenagers, and did the sulky bit with gusto. Don't all teenagers? And if they don't, where does that sulkiness go? Better to be a 'growing pain' when you're growing than later on in life when you're supposed to have a bit of maturity and common sense.

What class of a pain I was to my parents as a teenager, I don't know, but I do know the class of growing pains

I had – and they were type A for Awful. Being a female, they presented themselves on a regular basis, once a month from about the age of twelve and many's the day I would sit crouched on my bedroom floor in agony, unable to countenance the extent of the pain. I tell you, if anybody had offered to let me exchange those pains for a flurry of hot flushes, I'd have jumped at the opportunity!

My teenage years were not of the type you see on television in programmes like *Home and Away* that I sometimes catch a glimpse of as I'm passing through the TV room on the way to the kitchen. That's to be expected, I suppose. It's a while since I was a teenager. But my experience didn't even resemble the situations that were presented on television when I was that age. I remember being envious of Tammy in the programme of the same name on Teilifís Éireann, as it was called, an American import in the early seventies that I looked forward to every week. Tammy had clear skin, shiny long blonde hair, which was tied back in a ponytail, and a lithe athletic build. I was too young to refer to her build as her 'figure' in those days. Unlike Tammy, I had no figure, a straight down no-nonsense kind of body. I had a face full of freckles and my hair was mousey brown and frizzy. I felt that everyone was looking at me critically and I was convinced that everyone, even Tammy who, let's face it, didn't even exist in real life, had a better social life than me.

I was very shy, tall and awkward as a teenager. If anyone looked sideways at me, I'd blush bright red. My mother sent me to elocution lessons to give me a bit of confidence and to Irish dancing lessons because I walked with my toes turned it. I was a very serious and studious teenager. My children have decided I was a nerd. I'm glad to say that they have all come through their teenage years with much fonder memories of that time than I had. They have more of a sense of self and confidence which were in very short supply when I was that age.

It's comforting to know that there are others who have similar memories of their teenage years. I'm a great fan of Johnny Depp. He was great in movies like *Edward Scissorhands*, *Pirates of the Caribbean* and *Alice in Wonderland*. He has wonderful presence and charisma and is a fine actor. What do you think he has to say about his youth? It's not good!

"As a teenager, I was so insecure.
I was the type of guy that never fitted in
because he never dared to choose.
I was convinced I had
absolutely no talent at all. For nothing.
And that thought took away all my ambition."

JOHNNY DEPP

This from a man who went on to win Golden Globe and Screen Writers' Guild awards! And a man with whom I feel a bit of empathy because, although he's American, he is a Francophile and has bought himself a house with vineyard in Plan de la Tour, an idyllic spot in the south of France where I was an au pair/slave during my UCD days. I have written about that interlude in my life in *Paper Tigers*. Suffice it to say, I was employed as an au pair by a very wealthy French family who had a holiday estate in that little village up in the mountains above St Tropez. I was lonely as hell there and way out of my depth socially, given the lifestyle I was used to in Clondalkin, which, by the way, I wouldn't swap for their wealth or fabulous house and lifestyle. They were the type of people you'd be thinking of when you read this quotation from Andrew Young, former American politician and friend of Martin Luther King:

"Can wealth bring happiness?
Look around and see what gay distress!
Whatever fortunes lavishly can pour,
the mind annihilates and calls for more."

ANDREW YOUNG

Despite the beautiful surroundings, the vineyard, the swimming pool, the indoor and outdoor dining areas and palatial rooms, which I cleaned diligently before the arrival of guests from the worlds of business, film, politics, I actually don't think they were very happy. That was my perception as a twenty-year-old student. They were oblivious to the musings of William Wirt, the nineteenth-century American author, barrister and statesman whose words of wisdom I found in my mother's copybook of quotations.

"He is a great simpleton who imagines that
the chief power of wealth is to supply wants.
In ninety-nine cases out of a hundred it
creates more wants than it supplies."

William Wirt

Looking back now, I can see that they were always striving to impress, to be in with the 'in' crowd and bickering among themselves, seeking perfection – and we all know that's a pretty elusive commodity. When I was there as an au pair, they were the age I am now, so they should have known better, frankly! I am, however, glad I went there and had that very special insight into the French bourgeoisie, and if I had known that, in years to come, Johnny Depp would buy a place there, I would have savoured the experience in a totally different way! And I hope he savours that place of great natural beauty in a way that allows him to relax and enjoy it for what it is. And to be grateful to have the means to have such a place. He is obviously a very wealthy person and I hope he falls into the category described here by Donald Grant Mitchell:

"But wealth is a great means of refinement,
and it is a security for gentleness,
since it removes anxieties."

DONALD GRANT MITCHELL

Of all the stages of my life as a female, from child to teenager to adult and now to middle age, I think the time I was most fulfilled as a woman was during the years I was having my babies. I loved being pregnant. It was a time of great joy. When I was pregnant for the first time, I came across a piece in a mothering magazine and cut it out because it described exactly how I felt.

ꝺ

"A mother's joy begins when new life is stirring inside ... when a tiny heartbeat is heard for the first time, and a playful kick reminds her she is never alone."

ꝺ

For nine months, I felt well, energetic, excited. I couldn't wait to wear maternity dresses, even on my fourth pregnancy – and, in those days, we wore dresses! They were big and blousy, but I loved wearing them for what they signified. I was going to have a baby. I know I'm going to sound like something out of the Ark, but I have to admit I'm not a fan of the modern maternity wear which, as far as I can make out, is not maternity wear. I cannot see the appeal of a T-shirt or a top pulled across a huge belly with a baby inside and a belly button protruding through the cotton. It doesn't look comfortable and it doesn't look attractive. Okay, you can call me old fashioned!

I was lucky with each of my pregnancies because I never suffered with morning sickness and, after the first few weeks of tiredness which were highly acceptable because they were the signal that I was pregnant, I went into planning mode and was full of energy and activity. Planning didn't include buying anything for the baby – those were the days when the notion was that you'd be tempting fate if you had anything but the bare essentials for the birth (as laid down by the maternity hospital during the latter stages of the ante-natal visits). That was fine though. I took great pleasure in buying the babygros and marvelling at the tiny size of them and wondering was I really going to have a little one to put in them. With Eva, it was baby gowns that I brought into the Coombe. They were really sweet, made in brushed cotton with a little embroidered band from which came two lengths to tie a bow behind the back. Why any newborn baby needs a bow at the back of their gown beats me, but I was happy to tie that bow and have it just so when Eva arrived. I suppose I'm lucky my first was a girl in that case as I'm not sure Tom would thank me for talking about tying a bow for him as a baby (babygros had taken over from the gown by the time he came along).

I enjoyed being pregnant with every one of my for wonderful children. After Tom, my second child, was born, I miscarried a baby and that was a time of devastation. Every year on the anniversary of the miscarriage, I still remember the date and think of that baby who spent thirteen weeks inside me. I was very nervous during my next pregnancy, and was appalled when I seemed to be going down the route of miscarriage once again. There was a silver lining this time however because when I was taken in for a scan, the doctor was thrilled to be able to tell me that, yes, I had miscarried, but there was another healthy baby with a strong heartbeat visible on the screen. I had been carrying twins, and my now big strong twenty-one–year-old son, Eoin, arrived in October. Lucy was born eighteen months later.

I am eternally grateful that I had four healthy babies. Although I enjoyed every moment of pregnancy, I remember feeling very anxious at the moment of delivery, hoping and praying that everything would be okay. It's a moment of great worry and a seemingly interminable wait for the midwife and the paediatrician to complete their examination and utter those magic words to tell you that you have a strong, healthy baby. As Margaret Mead, the American anthropologist, a woman of great insight and wisdom, said:

"And when our baby stirs and struggles
to be born, it compels humility:
what we began is now its own."

MARGARET MEAD

❦

That is so true. Every woman is honoured and humbled by the miracle of giving birth, and grateful if our baby is strong. I have many, many friends whose babies were born healthy and not one of them has taken that gift for granted. I also have many friends who have given birth to babies who were less healthy or were born with some condition or disability. Each and every one of those mothers was heartbroken for the tiny person that might have to struggle in life. Each and every one of those mothers put their own heartache to one side and opened their heart and their arms even wider to mind that baby. That also is the miracle of childbirth. As Maureen Hawkins, the American poet, says:

❦

"Before you were conceived, I wanted you,
Before you were born, I loved you,
Before you were here an hour, I would die for you,
This is the miracle of Mother's Love."

Maureen Hawkins

❦

The third line says it all really. How often have you heard a parent say they would gladly swap places with their sick child? I know I would do anything at all for any of mine, and I know I'm just par for the course.

I was very happy and fulfilled being pregnant and caring for my babies. I've spoken about the trials of rearing small children already in Chapter 2, and how I'd like to think I'd do things differently if I had the time over. I'd take things at a slower pace, and look into their beautiful eyes more, and stroke their soft skin more, and run my hands through their hair while they're sleeping. The reality was, though, that through my own choice, I was juggling motherhood and a career and, therefore, while my children were sleeping, I wasn't running my fingers through their hair or stroking their skin, I was catching up on some chore that needed to be done or, when I was teaching, correcting copies and preparing the next day's classes. That stage of my life was action packed. There is a lot happening when there are four growing children in your life, developing their interests and their personalities. They need lots of care and attention. It was a period of my life that was filled with wonderful child-centred moments – the school plays, sports days, communions and confirmations.

It was also a period charged with different emotions. There was happiness. Who is not happy around children with their funny mannerisms, their energy, their angelic demeanour when they've finally fallen off to sleep after a whingey day? There was job satisfaction, especially having been chosen to present the Eurovision Song Contest in 1995, which was a great honour. There was sadness at the breakdown of my marriage and the death of my mother, my uncle and my cousin's wife in a relatively short space of time. My thirties and forties were a busy, busy stage of my life which gradually and naturally slowed down. For many years, I was like a whirling dervish, dropping children to school, going on to work, doing the supermarket shopping during my lunch break, presenting *Open House*, a live television programme, coming home to prepare dinner, checking homework, dropping and collecting for extracurricular activities, and so on and on. And do you know what? I loved it all. I thrive on being busy. The past couple of years, therefore, have been a period of major adjustment to a new stage in my life, with which I have struggled and with which I have finally come to terms. I have reached the point where I can see the sense of what Mother Teresa said about life and living:

"Be happy in the moment, that's enough.
Each moment is all we need, not more."

MOTHER TERESA

❧

I am happy in the moment now. I don't think too much about the future and what it holds and I don't hark back to the past. It wasn't always thus, however. As I described in Chapter 2, I reached a stage a few years ago where the children had all left school, were doing their own thing and didn't need me to be there. Good for them. I found I was superfluous. I had, horror of horrors, time on my hands, which took some getting used to. And I was entering middle age.

Whether we like it or not, for a woman, middle age equals menopause and menopause brings with it a sneaky bag of tricks that can turn a woman's life upside down. Some Smart Alec has devised a series of names for the '7 Dwarfs of Menopause'. They are: 'Itchy, Bitchy, Wrinkly, Sweaty, Sleepy, Bloated, Forgetful!'

It's funny to look at that list in print, not so funny to have to say it's quite an accurate description of the attributes of the 'Big M'. I have been told there are women who sail through the menopause without drawing breath. I was not one of them. I hated the onset of middle age, and I was never a fan of the hot flush. I know they've been referred to as 'power surges' but, believe me, when you're in an enclosed space, like a car, and you go from being cool, calm and collected to feeling this volcano of heat rising up inside you and bursting out of every pore, the only power I want is the strength to stick my fist through the window and shove my head out for a bit of cold air. I have also become forgetful to the point that my children have chosen my epitaph. My headstone will be adorned with the query: 'Has anyone seen my car keys?'

The Sleepy dwarf seems to have eluded me. I wouldn't mind falling prey to that symptom. My experience is of insomnia, which I put down to the fact that my night is a symphony of sweats. Enter Sweaty! As for Bitchy, I heard of a man who tried very hard to support his wife during the mood swings that were part of her experience of menopause. He bought her a mood ring which changed colour according to how she was feeling. When his wife was in a good mood, the stone in the ring turned green and when she was in a bad mood, it left a big red mark on his forehead. Joke! It's important to be able to laugh and have a sense of humour about these things.

I think it's fair to say that I was reluctant to embrace middle age and its attendant menopause, although now I am happy to accept that it's part of my being a woman – and I love being a woman. As I said at the beginning of this chapter though, I would have run a mile from writing about this stage of my life up to quite recently. I have asked myself why this was the case and, from the vantage point of acceptance of where and what I am now, I can honestly say that, like many women of my generation, I was caught in that trap of hanging on by my fingertips to the notion that if you don't admit to ageing, maybe it will go away.

The culture of youth, beauty and skinny minnies was at its zenith during the years of prosperity in this country. There was so much money floating about and so many opportunities to spend it that magazines were pushing an open door when they exhorted us all to be tall, thin, youthful, with long 'extensions-aided' flowing locks, figure-hugging expensive clothes and just plain expensive shoes, bags and jewellery. The fact that women come in all shapes and sizes and are of differing ages and have different tastes didn't matter a whit. We were all to look like Kate Moss or Angelina Jolie or Jennifer Aniston (if you really insisted on a bit of the girl-next-door look). We were to look like these or die in the attempt! Thankfully, along with the recession came a bit of common sense, perhaps its only recommendation. The atmosphere of near embarrassment that accompanied the realisation that we had become very materialistic during the boom times spilled over into the shallow culture of 'youth at all costs' and there has been a gradual shift in emphasis towards a more balanced view of life, living, and what's beautiful, what's worthwhile and what's sexy. And what's beautiful, worthwhile and sexy is not restricted to youth and the young.

There is no doubt that young women are stunningly beautiful. I look at my own two daughters, both in their twenties, and I see the beauty of their skin, their unlined faces, their shining hair and their good muscle tone. I also look at their eyes which are the window to the soul and I see that they have character and kindness which is in the formative stage and which will continue to grow and continue to flourish as they continue to age. On the other hand, that clear skin will fade, those unlined faces will become lined, the muscle tone will slacken. That is a fact of life. It is also a fact of life in the Western world that this human phenomenon has gone uncelebrated for a long time. Hidden. Reversed even. How many millions of euro, pounds and dollars have been spent by women trying to turn back the clock? How many times have you come across a product or a procedure that claimed to 'halt the signs of ageing'? The message has always been that it is not good for a woman to age and the people for whom that message had the strongest impact have always been the women in their middle years, the women who have left youth and all that entails behind them.

Middle age has been a difficult time for women. They were neither one thing nor the other. So many women felt they were becoming invisible. I'm no different to anyone else. I got a bit of a fright when I started noticing lines, under my eyes to begin with, probably in my late thirties, early forties. Now I've got so used to them, I just look to see how deep this year's batch is. And I nod in agreement and approval every time I read Mark Twain's little gem:

"Wrinkles should merely indicate where smiles have been."
MARK TWAIN

There was a time, though, when I was hanging on to the ideal of the elixir of youth, railing against the changes taking place in my body, looking backwards, rather than enjoying this middle stage in life, with all its gifts and all its challenges. So what happened to change my mindset? When did it become okay to be middle aged and proud? Like I said, the recession, which of course has been very difficult in so many ways, did bring with it a way of thinking and a way of being that are less superficial – less bling, less shallow, more real. We've all begun to appreciate the good things more, things of substance that we enjoy in this life, things like relationships, health and well being. And with that appreciation came confidence and a self-esteem that, for many women, myself included, had started to wane with the advent of middle age.

And there's nothing like the menopause to let you know for certain you're entering a different stage in life. It's a tough old adversary which can play with your head and your feelings just as strongly as it can have you, without any prior notice, resembling a tomato that's just been immersed in a pot of boiling water so that you can peel it more easily! Gradually I began to realise that boiling tomatoes are beautiful too. And funny. And wise. And sexy even. I'd rather spend an evening chatting with one of those boiling tomatoes who had something to say for herself than with an Angelina Jolie or a Kate Moss lookalike who just looked good. And that seems to be the way of things more and more. So many middle-aged women are 'bien dans sa peau' – happy in their skin. Those who still need to be convinced of this should ponder for a while the positive words of Margaret Mead, a champion of women at every age.

"There is no more creative force in the world than the menopausal woman with zest."

MARGARET MEAD

Way to go, Margaret. In my own case, when I had accepted this new stage in life and acknowledged the sadness that I am no longer the centre of the universe for my children, I could embrace life in a whole new way. I am free to go places without watching the clock to be home at a certain time. I am travelling to new places, meeting new people, thinking new thoughts. I am a menopausal woman with zest! I am also a realist and I will continue to hate the flushes and the sweats, despite the fact that they provide amusement for my children as I rush to open the door of the fridge for some cold air and through their laughter, they ask me, 'Are ya boilin', Mum?' Very funny! I remind my daughters that 'it's all before them' and my sons that they will experience it from the other supportive side, hopefully without acquiring a few red marks on the forehead from a mood ring! I will continue to exercise and go to Pilates, which is fantastic for toning and flexibility. I will continue to be careful about what I eat Monday to Friday and enjoy gatherings with friends at the weekends. I love life and this is where I am in life at the moment. Brigitte Bardot described ageing well and, let's face it, she had a lot to lose in middle age, having been such a stunningly beautiful woman in her younger days:

"It's sad to grow old, but nice to ripen."

Brigitte Bardot

❧

It's nice to enjoy life at its different stages. It's a blessing to be healthy and active and it's important to take steps to maintain health and fitness with good exercise and diet.

To finish this chapter where it began, when we encounter people who have gone past middle age and are in their later years, it behoves us to respect all the other stages they have lived and the contributions they have made during their lives. They deserve that dignity and regard that is so visible in other cultures and sadly lacking in our own. Just as every young, beautiful woman will enter middle age, unless tragedy strikes, so too under the same circumstance will every middle-aged person enter old age. My wish is that we embrace each different stage of life with enthusiasm, energy and joie de vivre and that people will say of us, in the words of Oliver Wendell Holmes, the nineteenth-century Harvard professor and poet:

❧

"For him in vain the envious seasons roll,
Who bears eternal summer in his soul."

Memories are Made of This

"We ask for long life, but 'tis deep life,
or noble moments that signify.
Let the measure of time be spiritual,
not mechanical."

RALPH WALDO EMERSON

When a person reaches an acceptance of the middle stage of life, those words, penned by the nineteenth-century American essayist and poet Ralph Waldo Emerson, take on a very real significance. I outlined my own journey to this point of acceptance in Chapter 4 and while I certainly look forward to long life, I also look forward to that long life being interesting, exciting, challenging, satisfying and fun. I want it to be deep and full of noble moments. Not asking for much, am I? Perhaps I am, but I think it's a valid aspiration. I realise that if I want that kind of a life, I have to play my part. I also know that there is a very wise saying about God disposing while man is proposing. As Hamlet said to Horatio:

"There's a divinity that shapes our ends
Rough-hew them how we will."

HAMLET

I accept that I am not the mistress of my destiny in terms of how long I will live, but I am mistress of the efforts I can make to be healthy, fulfilled and happy for however long I am on this earth. Now that I am looking at a new stage in life, where I can take more time to myself, I want to use that time well and to be conscious of the many good things I have and to nurture them well. I also have the possibility of embarking on adventures that were impossible before. Nuala O'Faolain brought that realisation home to me with a sentence in her book *Best Love, Rosie*:

"You face both ways now. You can reach back to vigour, and forward to wisdom."

NUALA O'FAOLAIN

Certainly, the years to date have been lived with vigour. It would have been difficult for them to be otherwise, raising four lively youngsters. The house was full of noise and friends, and that gave me great joy. I loved having their pals over for parties and sleepovers. I'm a firm believer in the importance of building up lots of memories during those special years. Cicero said:

"Memory is the treasury and guardian of all things."

CICERO

I always strove to fill my children's lives with good memories. And I hope that they will go on to provide the same for their children. Birthdays are very special times in a family. I think they should be marked simply, but with lots of fuss. I know that might sound like a contradiction in terms but it's not. It's possible to create a simple but memorable and happy celebration. No need to go overboard, no need to break the bank. And such fun to be had.

I remember birthday parties that my mother organised for me when I was growing up. I don't remember the details of my brothers' or sister's parties and I think that is the essence of a party well organised. The celebrant remembers the day in a special way because he or she was the centre of attention and made to feel very special. There are people who never have a fuss made of them, and I think that's sad. I remember the parties, the balloons, the cards and the food. I don't remember the presents, and I think that's a further indication that it's the gathering of friends and family that make the occasion special – and the party food. We had butterfly buns (fairy cakes with the top sliced off and made into wings, fixed in position by jam and cream!), jelly and the pièce de résistance was always the ice-cream cake. We had party bags too. They might only have a balloon, a biro and a few loose sweets in them, but they were sought after and treasured. We were easily pleased for sure and isn't it nice for that to be the case. I am sure my mother fell into a heap of exhaustion at the end of those parties but I carry the memory still and have always made an effort to get the excitement level high for my children as they had their friends over for birthday parties. They are wonderful occasions.

"A birthday is the first day of another 365-day journey around the sun."

Isn't that a nice way to view a birthday, a sunny time of adventure and happiness? I really enjoyed preparing for my children's birthday parties. I was a dab hand at making traffic light cookies (shortbread with a dollop of red, orange and green icing) and orange boats (orange skins cut in quarters, filled with orange jelly and left to set, then adorned with a cocktail stick and a triangle of white paper, for the sail of course!). Rice Krispie buns are self-explanatory and always a big hit with little ones, and then there would be a different cake design for each year. But of course! Did you ever see the same gown going down the catwalk in Paris or Milan two seasons in a row? Some of the cakes that adorned my children's birthday tables, and led to a series of 'wows' from the pals, were a red post box and a Thomas the Tank engine, both of which were made in empty tomato cans that deputised very nicely as cake moulds. Also featured on occasions were a cute sponge rabbit, covered in coconut, a Maypole sponge with a straw in the middle and coloured streamers out to each side of the cake and a record, by Kylie Minogue actually! Lots of chocolate-flavoured butter icing on the top of the cake and ridges for the grooves and a simple circle of white paper with the name of the song in the middle. Simple all of them, but great fun to make. I almost forgot the Minnie Mouse cake but that was made in a special mould bought in Disneyland, so it was trouble free.

I hope the children have happy memories of those parties and the excitement of the occasions and that those memories will stay with them and make them realise how much they are loved, as J.M. Barrie says:

"God gave us memories that we might have roses in December."

J.M. Barrie

I think I got as much fun out of those birthday parties as the children did. We still celebrate them all, every year, with cards, a cake and candles. It's getting to the stage, though, where you'd nearly need to have a fire extinguisher to hand with the number of candles on the cakes. Lighting them has become a two-person job, otherwise the first ones would have burned away to nothing by the time the last ones were lit, especially in the case of *my* birthday!

It's not just birthdays that I like to celebrate. I'm a sucker for other times of the year as well. I have an attic full of decorations – and they're not all red and green and Santa themed either. I begin my campaign of celebration and decoration in February with St Valentine's Day. This is quite an understated occasion with some very tasteful red furry cushions, some heart-shaped paper chains, fake red rose petals and, of course, red candles. You have to have candles. I'd have more paraphernalia to display, but the pound shops weren't big on Valentine's decorations when I was building up my stock. St Patrick's Day is next, a time when the red paper chains make way for green shamrock-shaped ones, hanging leprechauns and a few green wigs and hats, left over from the glory days of following the Irish soccer team in the World Cup.

I love our Easter decorations. I would describe them as classy. Many of my friends would describe them in other terms but they are definitely a bit more salubrious than the ones that have preceded them in the calendar. I have a collection of Easter wreaths, including a big green and yellow one for the hall door, a tree on which I hang Easter decorations and there's the odd furry chick and cutesie bunny to dot around the mantelpiece and the shelves. I love Easter. There's a feeling of hope and light associated with the season, a celebration of life and the end of Lent. As Samuel Dickey Gordon, who wrote a series of book on spiritual matters entitled *Quiet Talks* put it:

"Easter spells out beauty,
the rare beauty of new life."

SAMUAL DICKEY GORDON

ꝶ

There seems to me to be a gentleness in the writings about Easter and that time of the year. I suppose for us it begins in the Celtic tradition with St Brigid's Day and the start of spring:

ꝶ

"Anois teacht an earraigh,
beidh an lá ag dul chun síneadh,
Is tar éis na Féile Bríde, ardóidh mé mo sheol."

Ó RAIFTEIRÍ

ꝶ

Those words from Ó Raifteirí's poem about spring and St Brigid's Day and the stretch in the evenings found favour with both Brian Cowen and Enda Kenny on the occasion of the dissolution of the Dáil on 1 February

2011. It was lovely to hear Irish poetry recited in the Dáil chamber, and that gentleness associated with poems about spring and Easter time is just as lovely in the Irish language as in English. One of my favourite poems about Easter time is A.E. Housman's 'Loveliest of Trees, the Cherry Now'. Every time I look at my Easter hall door wreath with its tiny white cloth blossoms I think of these lines.

"Loveliest of trees, the cherry now
Is hung with bloom along the bough,
And stands about the woodland ride
Wearing white for Eastertide."

A.E. Housman

There's nothing pretty or sweet about Hallowe'en in my house. It's in a league of its own with ghosts and ghouls and witches everywhere, some of whom cackle and scream as you pass by. Scary, in a nice way! I justify the number of Hallowe'en decorations in the house by virtue of the fact that both Tom and Eoin have their birthdays at the end of October, and it would be terrible not to mark the occasion with a bit of tack – sorry, colour! And as for Christmas … there's hardly room for us in the house with the number of decorations – and I love every one of them. They help to maintain the cosy and warm atmosphere that I want for the house and the people who come through the door over the holiday period, the kind of atmosphere described by Sir Walter Scott:

"Heap on more wood!
The wind is chill;
But let it whistle as it will,
We'll keep our Christmas merry still."

Sir Walter Scott

Each year, I swear I will buy no more decorations. And each year, after Christmas, I succumb and buy a few bits in the January sales. I find it hard to resist a bargain! My children call me the 'Queen of Tack'. When it comes to decorating the house for Christmas, I know no bounds. I have the decorations the children made when they were in primary school. I have Christmas decorations from my travels to different countries – Lapland Santa, Polish Santa, Canadian Santa, beautiful glass baubles from Poland and the Czech Republic, a wooden crib from Malawi, and that's just the start of it. I have boxes and bags of every type of traditional decoration you could mention. It takes a couple of days to decorate the house before Christmas and I enjoy it all. I'm not so fond of taking them all down and putting them away on 6 January but, all in all, it's worth it. I subscribe to the thoughts outlined here by Lenora Mattingly Weber:

"Christmas is a time for children. But it is for grown-ups too. Even if it is a headache, a chore, and nightmare, it is a period of necessary defrosting of chill and hide-bound hearts."

LENORA MATTINGLY WEBER

I'm more than willing to do my bit to help in the defrosting of any chill hearts around Christmas time. I reckon my decorated and well-lit house and garden bear testimony to that. I've often wondered why I continue to decorate the house for the different occasions during the year. There's no doubt it involves a lot of work and can be a bit of a pain when you have to take everything down again and pack it away. I've come to the conclusion that there are two reasons for my diligence. I'm a traditionalist at heart and I like to continue doing the things that I enjoyed doing and the children enjoyed seeing as they were growing up. We're very lucky in this country to have a rich heritage of traditional observances to mark different times of the year. Maybe this is my twenty-first-century attempt at hanging on to some of them. Nobody will ever persuade me that St Brigid's Day is not the first day of spring. I know that there are geographical and meteorological reasons for thinking otherwise but as Tevye says in *Fiddler on the Roof*, 'it's tradition'!

"Because of our traditions, we have kept our balance for many years.
Because of our traditions, every one of us knows exactly who he is ...
Without our traditions, our lives would be as shaky as a fiddler on the roof."

Now I'm not suggesting we should all go back to living as they did in the days of Tsarist Russia, as depicted in that wonderful musical where Papa read the Holy Book,

Mama did all the household chores and the daughters learned to clean, cook and mend while the sons were educated. And all the while, everyone was keeping an eye out for a man standing precariously on a roof while playing a fiddle! It is a wonderful musical with lots of great moments of song and comedy. I love the part where the old Rabbi recites his prayer for the Tsar:

"God bless the Tsar and keep him [long pause] far away from us!"

Tradition and humour were certainly key concepts for Tevye and company in *Fiddler on the Roof*. It's interesting, I think, that there are echoes of those concepts in our own traditions when you look for instance at Yeats' poem 'The Fiddler of Dooney':

"When I play on my fiddle in Dooney,
Folk dance like a wave of the sea."

W.B. YEATS

A lovely image there of the traditional fiddler setting up – hopefully not on a roof – and making people happy. In fact, the fiddler seems pretty content with the service he's providing for the community at large. So much so, he reckons that:

ᘓ

"When we come at the end of time
To Peter sitting in state,
He will smile on the three old spirits,
But call me first through the gate."

W.B. YEATS

ᘓ

Two of the three old spirits are his brother and his cousin, who are priests. They won't be top of the queue. The fiddler will be up there, though, probably entertaining the souls in heaven:

ᘓ

"For the good are always the merry,
Save by an evil chance,
And the merry love the fiddle,
And the merry love to dance."

W.B. YEATS

Back to St Brigid. There are lovely customs associated with her feast day, which are uniquely Irish. Each year, my sister Deirdre brings us a blessed Brigid's Cross which I hang in the hallway. The previous year's cross is removed and burned on the fire. That's the only observance I make each year, but I know there are many more celebrated around the country, particularly in places associated with St Brigid, places like Faughart in County Louth where she was born and Kildare town where she built her church. Deirdre and I have a particular affection for St Brigid because there's a Brigid's well in Clondalkin where we grew up. And the story goes that a well sprang up in places where Brigid spent the night on her way to Kildare to seek land for a church.

The road where we grew up was St Brigid's Road. When we were at school, also called after St Brigid, the custom was that a group of pupils would be sent to the well before her feast day to clean it up. The tally of rubbish often included shopping trolleys, old boots, sticks and papers. It was a dirty job, but the place always looked well (pardon the pun!) on 1 February. I notice that the well is tended and looking its best at all times of the year now, a testament to community spirit and a good army of volunteers. Other traditions associated with the feast day include St Brigid's Mantle, a piece of white material that used to be tied to a bush or tree on the eve of St Brigid's Day for her to bless as she travelled the land accompanied by her white cow with red ears. There's also the tradition of the Brideog, a doll dressed in white garments and carried from house to house. I find the prayer of St Brigid uplifting:

"I would like the angels of heaven to be among us.
I would like an abundance of peace.
I would like full vessels of charity.
I would like rich treasures of mercy.
I would like cheerfulness to preside over all."

St Brigid

Aspirations that are as valid and meaningful today as they must have been in Brigid's time way back in sixth-century Ireland.

Our male patron saint, Patrick, has, of course, customs and traditions associated with his feast day that have not only endured in this country but all around the world wherever the Irish gather. I don't imagine that's going to change any time soon. There's one aspect of St Patrick's Day traditions that brings me right back to my childhood when the day began with donning the shamrock and the green ribbons in our hair (only the girls of course, the boys were spared this observance). Then off to Mass and singing along with the choir:

"Hail, glorious Saint Patrick, dear saint of our isle,
On us thy poor children bestow a sweet smile;
And now thou art high in the mansions above,
On Erin's green valleys look down in thy love."

Sr Agnes

There's no doubting the power of music to evoke memories and I'm sure those lines above will be a strong reminder for many people my age of the lives we lived growing up in Ireland in the sixties and before. I also have a soft spot for a hymn in Irish to St Patrick, which I taught to my Irish students every year in the weeks before 17 March.

"Dóchas linn Naomh Pádraig,
Aspal mór na hÉireann,
Ainm oirearc gléigeal,

solas mór an tsaoil é.
D'fhill le soiscéal grá dúinn
d'ainneoin blianta i ngéibheann.
Grá mór Mhac na Páirte,
d'fhuascail cách ón daorbhraid."

TOMÁS Ó FLANNGHAILE

There are lovely melodies in both the Irish and the English versions of the hymn to St Patrick. And I'm delighted to say that when I was teaching Irish to secondary school students, they were always enthusiastic about learning 'Dóchas Linn' as we affectionately referred to it. Mind you that was more than twenty years ago. I'm not so sure the same would be true of students nowadays. I know my own children don't know the words any more. What a pity that we treat those unique and worthy elements of our culture so lightly.

I've already spoken of the customs my parents subscribed to around Easter time. There was a lot of time spent washing windows and floors and weeding gardens and visiting the church. The recompense was being allowed to wear ankle socks from Easter Sunday right through the summer. Easter in modern times has embraced some traditions from other countries and cultures, a bit more pleasing to the younger folk I think. When my children were small, they really enjoyed painting hard-boiled eggs and displaying them over Easter. I never did that as a child. The Easter Bunny visited before they rose on Easter Sunday and left sweets and chocolate everywhere, inside and outside the house. Not in my day! We got one chocolate egg each and we made it last I can tell you. I don't ask my children to wash the windows for Easter, but I do like the house to be bright and so I spring clean it before then. I always cook lamb that day and I have been known to make an Easter cake in a wonderful lamb cake mould I bought on holiday in Germany. Out comes the coconut again. It serves equally well as lamb's wool as it did in earlier days for rabbit fur!

I think it's fair to say that I am a traditionalist at all times of the year, from spring through summer to Hallowe'en and Christmas, and observing the customs and traditions and taking out the decorations ticks that box very nicely. Also, I just love my home. I'm always on the lookout for things that will enhance it and I like it to look different at different times of the year. My house looks very different at Christmas and at other festival times. My home is the place where I am most comfortable and where I love to welcome friends. All the effort of putting up the decorations would be for nothing if I only did it for me. I love having friends around at any time. Emerson, who had a very warm view of life, put it in a nutshell when he said:

"The ornament of a house is the friends who frequent it."

RALPH WALDO EMERSON

There is no nicer way to spend free time than in the company of friends, to welcome them into your home or to visit them in theirs. I love to sit and chat with friends in the garden in the summer and by the fire in the winter. I love to cook for my friends, to set a nice table and to sit and eat and have an informal evening of food and wine and conversation. I enjoy the planning, the preparation, organising the finishing touches. I want my friends to come in the hall door to a feeling of warmth and welcome because I agree wholeheartedly with Antoine de Saint-Exupéry, the author of *Le Petit Prince*, when he said:

"There is no hope of joy except in human relations."

ANTOINE DE SAINT-EXUPÉRY

❧

Up to quite recently, all meals in my house were served at the big pine table in the kitchen. Why? Because I didn't have a dining-room suite. I did have a dining room but used it as a study with the computer, printer and various book cases taking up the space. I was very happy with that arrangement and enjoyed entertaining guests in the kitchen. I did try to position them in a strategic manner with their backs to the sink and cooker so they would be spared having to look at the bombsite that was the preparation area. A sink is not a pretty sight at the best of times and certainly not when it's full of pots, pans, bowls and whatever else had been used to prepare the culinary delights being enjoyed. To be fair to my friends and family, none of them would ever be bothered by anything like that. And neither would I visiting another's home for dinner. It's about the company, the sharing of a meal in a relaxed atmosphere. There was a plaque hanging in our kitchen at home when I was growing up, an oval-shaped piece of wood with a picture of a woman baking on it and the caption read:

❧

"No matter where I serve my guests.
It seems they like my kitchen best."

A friend of my mother's brought it home from holiday for her, and the irony is that Mam always served her guests in the 'good room'. Those were the days when friends came after tea and sat around the fire chatting, with supper served around ten o'clock. Supper consisted of tea and dainty sandwiches served on nice bone china plates with doyleys and a cake with less butter icing in it than might have been expected. (The reason for diminished butter icing will follow later.)

I also have a plaque hanging in my kitchen, also a gift from a friend. It reads:

"The smoke alarm went off … dinner's ready!"

No laughing! In my defence, I must say that the oven is very low in my kitchen and the smoke alarm goes off at the drop of a hat! I like cooking and I have become more proficient and more adventurous now that I have more time to experiment. I think that sharing a nice meal with friends is one of life's pleasures, and there have been many instances of that pleasure in the kitchen of this house over the years and in the garden when the weather allows. I've got quite clever on that score and invested in a canopy which can be rolled out to cover the patio if, heaven forbid, there might be a shower of rain during a summer barbecue. I feel privileged to have had those happy gatherings and I look forward to many more in the years to come. We do well to remember the words of the nineteenth-century French author Charles Pierre Monselet:

"Ponder well on this point: the pleasant hours of our life are all connected by a more or less tangible link, with some memory of the table."

CHARLES PIERRE MONSELET

Up to last year, those pleasant hours of my life were connected with very informal memories of the table. Then my brother John asked me if I would like to take our parents' dining-room suite. It had been stored in his house since our mother died and it wasn't being used. I wasn't sure I had the space for it either, but I wasn't ready to see it leave the family so, after much huffing and puffing caused by the carting of tables and chairs and the subsequent relocation of computer and bookcases in rooms upstairs, I took possession of the dining-room suite that had been a wedding present to my mother and father and had been a fixture in the dining room in St Brigid's Road for almost fifty years.

I was not prepared for the journey down memory lane that ensued, precipitated by an art deco-style lacquered sideboard, table and six chairs. No sooner had I started putting my cutlery and crockery into the sideboard than I remembered what used to be on the different shelves as we were growing up. The top of the sideboard was where Mam placed her cakes once they were iced. When she wasn't looking, I used to lift the top layer and scrape off loads of the butter icing with my finger, being careful to avoid the sides because it would be noticed if they were a bit sparse. Coffee-flavoured icing was my favourite. I don't think she ever realised that her guests were eating scrumptious cakes that were a bit dry in the middle. I hope they didn't think she was being mean with the icing! At Christmas time, the sideboard would be adorned with up to six Christmas cakes waiting to be given to family and friends as presents. They weren't interfered with. I don't know how

to rob icing off a Christmas cake without it showing. Memories of family meals came flooding back as soon as I sat on the squeaky chair. We always tried to avoid sitting on that one. It was usually assigned to Tony because, being the youngest, he was also the lightest. The table is quite narrow and barely accommodates its six chairs so when there were visitors, the top of a table-tennis table was laid on top and, do you know what – the first thing I bought after I took possession of the suite was a large piece of MDF to serve the same purpose. Like mother, like daughter! I am so pleased that the dining-room suite, that my mother cherished and polished and covered so we couldn't scratch it, is alive and well and living in my house, facilitating happy gatherings and keeping alive some very happy memories of former times. I've already quoted this lovely line by J.M. Barrie, the man who created Peter Pan, it's one I particularly like:

"God gave us memories so that we might have roses in December."

J.M. Barrie

The memories that have sprung up since the arrival of the family dining-room suite are certainly a rose in the December of loss that endures after the death of parents and the end of happy childhood days. I love having it here and I admire the craftsmanship that went into its manufacture, the tongued and grooved drawers covered in green baize for the cutlery, the shiny lacquer finish. It really is a nice piece of furniture. I have to admit though that when I was young, I thought it was the most old-fashioned thing imaginable. I had no regard for its finesse whatsoever. In fact, I had no regard for having a dining room and while I still love having a crowd of people eating a 'one pot wonder' around the kitchen table, there's something special about the dining room as well. What do you think that says about me, I wonder? That I'm at that middle stage of life. And that I'm happy with all that entails, including embracing the niceties of a second-hand dining-room suite from the fifties.

I have time, now that my children are older, to experiment with new recipes and cook things from scratch in an unhurried way. Long gone are the weekends when I liquidised a selection of meat and veg mixtures for the following week for the babies. I'm still liquidising but it's soups and smoothies these days. I get great pleasure from having a big pot of soup on the cooker ready to feed anyone who comes in. I use home-made stock from chicken carcases and legs of lamb. Very simple, but people seem to like them and they're zero points! Anyone who has ever dieted will know what I mean by that little reference. We'll discuss the dreaded 'D' word in a different chapter; for the moment, suffice it to say that I enjoy feeding people. It's the nurturing side of my personality coming to the fore in a different way I suppose, now that I no longer need to nurture by washing and clothing and kissing pains away. I am certainly facing both ways now in the way described by Nuala O'Faolain at the beginning of this chapter. I may be looking back to vigour, but am I looking forwards to wisdom? I suppose it's a bit early to know that yet. I am looking forward with enthusiasm for sure.

After all that talk of tables and dinners, I think it might be nice now to ponder in the following pages the joys and the dilemmas of food – the feasts, the diets, the place food has in my life. Fran Lebowitz, that witty and irreverent American observer of humanity and society, put it well:

"Food is an important part of a balanced diet."

FRAN LEBOWITZ

There are occasions when food and balance seem at opposite ends of the spectrum. People may be surprised to realise that I could write an anthology about diets and dieting. I've tried them all and the sad thing is that I am not somebody who 'struggled with her weight'. I didn't have extra weight as a youngster, but I got sucked into the trap of wanting to lose a pound or two and wanting to look different. I'm annoyed with myself for letting that mentality take hold, because I know now that it took a lot of the joy out of food for me for many years. More of that in the following pages. Let's end this chapter on a positive note, remembering once again the happiness my home and my family bring me. I love putting the key in the door. My house is my sanctuary, a place where I can be me and where I want people to be relaxed, comfortable, well fed and totally unstressed.

There was another plaque on the wall in my family home in Clondalkin. It seemed very old fashioned to me as I was growing up, a bit like the dining-room suite that I now treasure. I can relate to the sentiments expressed now in the words of 'Bless This House', which had pride of place in our kitchen in Clondalkin:

"Bless this house, O Lord, we pray,
Make it safe by night and day ..."

HELEN TAYLOR

ꝏ

'Bless This House' was written in 1927 by Helen Taylor and May H. Morgan and there's no doubt that times have changed. We are far more sophisticated in our twenty-first-century homes with all mod cons that wouldn't have seemed possible to them almost a hundred years ago. I remember my mother taking out the washing machine into the centre of the kitchen every Monday and the windows steaming up as the water bubbled and she fed the wet clothes through a manual wringer. I wouldn't dream of having my washing machine or dryer in the kitchen even. They're in the shed because I don't have a utility room. I'd prefer the walk around to the shed than having to listen to the machines whirring. There'd be no living with me if I had to take the washing machine out into the middle of the kitchen floor and turn a handle to drain the water from the clothes before hanging them out on the line in the back garden! I transfer them from one machine to another, the dryer sits on top of the washing machine. In my defence, I must say that I love hanging clothes outdoors to dry and I like the sight of a line full of washing blowing in the wind; however, on the many occasions when it's lashing rain, I have the option of the automatic dryer, something that my mother did not.

There are many other labour-saving devices in the domestic arena nowadays, but the basic notions contained in 'Bless This House' are still of paramount importance. The first wish is for a safe house, a sanctuary for the people therein. The prayer continues with very fundamental requests for sound and wholesome qualities:

"Bless these walls so firm and stout,
Keeping want and trouble out ...
Bless the roof and chimney tall
Let thy peace lie over all ..."

HELEN TAYLOR

Who doesn't want to have a peaceful house, a trouble-free house? The final two lines of the first stanza though are my favourites. They remind me of something my brother John said at our mother's funeral. She died at Christmas 2001, and her funeral Mass was held on 27 December. At the end of the Mass, John thanked people for coming to pay their respects and for their support.

He invited everyone back to my mother's house in St Brigid's Road for soup and sandwiches. We had decided to have the gathering there because Mam always loved having people into her home. As he said from the altar, 'Mam had an Open House before it was ever a television programme on RTÉ', a reference to the programme I was presenting with Marty Whelan at the time. My wish is that others feel that my house is an open house and that it embodies the sentiments in these lines from 'Bless This House'. In fact, I'd like to have them put on a plaque and hung on the wall in my kitchen:

"Bless the door that it may prove,
Ever open,
To joy and love."

HELEN TAYLOR

Food, Glorious Food

"Roses are red,
Violets are blue,
Sugar is sweet
And so are you."

It is St Valentine's Day as I write this. It also happens to be a Monday, which is not the best day of the week for celebrations so I decided to have a Valentine's dinner yesterday for my children and the various boyfriends and girlfriends. What was the first item on the preparatory agenda? Got it in one! The bag of decorations came down from the attic and I enjoyed hanging the red hearts from the ceiling, putting out the red tablecloth with hearts and little xs (for kisses, of course) and sprinkling heart-shaped confetti on it just in case anyone was in any doubt as to the theme of the day! I found a few cute little bears in the bag along with a cheeky red devil teddy and a pair of red furry handcuffs, or love cuffs to give them their correct title. I can't remember which of my children brought those into the house. I suppose I should be thankful they were still in their box! I put a little Valentine's gift at every place, but the pièce de résistance was as always the placing of the two large furry heart-shaped cushions. If this is beginning to sound tasteless and tacky to you as you read, you've got the picture.

It *is* tacky but it's fun and bright and cheerful, and I love the look on people's faces when they come into a room that I have decorated for an occasion. It's usually a mixture of surprise and acceptance, evenly divided between the people who are witnessing this transformation of a perfectly fine kitchen into a haven of hearts for the first time (they're the surprised ones) and those, family included of course, who are well used to my penchant for decorations and such like. They just throw their eyes up to heaven and ask what's for dinner! The food doesn't escape the dreaded theme-park effect either. To begin, while watching the Six Nations clash between Ireland and France at Lansdowne Road, which was exciting and frustrating, particularly in the latter stages, we sat and nibbled on guacamole which Eva had made, nice and spicy for Valentine's Day! She adhered to the colour scheme by including red peppers and carrots, and the spicy trend continued with the main course which was a joint of spiced beef which I had had in the freezer since Christmas. That was accompanied by winter vegetables and roast potatoes served in a heart-shaped casserole dish. Dessert was strawberry cheesecake and Eva made a chocolate cake in a heart-shaped mould and covered it with red butter icing. I resisted the temptation to help myself to some of the icing, particularly as it was all over the top of the cake and would have looked a bit obvious. I admit it all sounds like a bit of a mish mash of tastes and flavours. It was, and the reason I have detailed the different elements of the meal is to show that, for me, the joy of cooking is the fact that it brings people together in a convivial atmosphere. I agree wholeheartedly with Ina Garten, former White House nuclear analyst and food guru known as the Barefoot Contessa:

"Food is not about impressing people.
It's about making them feel comfortable."

INA GARTEN

We had a lovely Valentine's celebration yesterday. I know I'll remember it with fondness and I hope my children will also and that there will be many more similar occasions. Sure isn't St Patrick's Day just around the corner! I can see it already. Guacamole would fit the bill perfectly again with perhaps green and yellow peppers. There'd have to be bacon and cabbage on the menu and I must make sure I have green food colouring in stock for the cakes and buns!

The fact that I enjoy those mixum gatherum culinary experiences is not to say that I don't enjoy fine dining as well. I love going to restaurants and always choose dishes that I wouldn't eat at home, dishes that are unusual or complicated. It's a great opportunity to be adventurous and I will try most things. I love fish and crab meat is a firm favourite, but I have a blind spot when it comes to mussels and oysters. I had a bad experience with mussels once and as for oysters, I'm afraid I just don't get them. I have tried but I have got no pleasure from feeling a live jelly-like substance sliding down my throat and chewing on sand and grit afterwards. As Jonathan Swift said:

"He was a brave man who first ate an oyster."

JONATHAN SWIFT

Brave certainly, or desperate perhaps. I am lucky never to be desperately hungry and my bravery does not extend to eating oysters.

We are lucky in this country to have lots of lovely restaurants. Many of them are overpriced compared to ones we visit when we're abroad, and the fact that very fine restaurants are closing down in these tough times bears testimony to that. There are very creative people working in the food industry in this country. We are, as a race, creative by nature, whether it be literature, music, gardening or cooking. We are also hospitable by nature, so the combination should naturally make for great dining experiences. And, in many cases, in many parts of the country, it does. There is something really special about a nice meal in a restaurant where there is a relaxed atmosphere, a bit of a buzz, interesting décor and innovative food. We've certainly come a long way from the dining room in Clery's or the Gresham where special occasions were celebrated when I was a child. They were the posh places and we generally got to go there once a year, for an anniversary or a Christmas treat perhaps. More often, we would have a Knickerbocker Glory in Cafolla's on O'Connell Street and that was the best of fun too. We've also come a long way from being happy with any meal in a restaurant because it's being 'served up to ya'. My mother and father were very easy going in that regard. They rarely ate out and, even in her later years, if you asked Mam what the meal she'd had was like, she'd say it was fine, nice not to have to cook, nice to have it served up.

We are far more discerning nowadays, and rightly so. I said we were a hospitable and creative race by nature but there are times when that creativity and hospitality can be in short supply to the customer, and that is so wrong. Particularly with the high prices we pay in restaurants in this country. Last September, I spent a weekend with friends on a cruiser on the Shannon and visited a riverside restaurant which was bedecked with badges and awards, but which, in the opinion of our group, was sadly lacking in the most basic of areas. The restaurant was housed in a lovely old stone building with a big open fire in the bar area. There is nothing more welcoming than a blazing fire but, alas, the fire wasn't lit even though it was six o'clock in the evening in late September. You could perhaps overlook that because the grate was filled with lots of white candles of different heights and thickness. A nice collection but, guess what … they weren't lighting either. Most uninviting and inhospitable. Drinks were ordered, but there was no ice – there was a problem with the freezer. Fair enough, but there were plenty of ice buckets on top of the bar and there was a pub across the road. The food was good but the dining experience was ruined by the lack of warmth with the fire episode

and the lack of chill with the ice episode. Such a shame when you consider the number of people who would disembark from their boat having spent a day on the Shannon and looking forward to a good meal in a cosy place by the river. They would be sorely disappointed in this establishment and I hope it wouldn't dissuade them from trying other eateries along the river. To quote Samuel Johnson:

"The finest landscape in the world is improved by a good inn in the foreground."

SAMUEL JOHNSON

There are great places to eat all along the Shannon, from pubs like The Purple Onion in Tarmonbarry where they serve wonderful home-made burgers, great chips and salads, to establishments like The Wineport in Glasson, just outside Athlone where the service, food and ambience all combine to make it a place to remember. There's another reason why it's memorable, and I'll deal with that presently.

People eat out for a variety of reasons, but no matter what the circumstances of the visit to the restaurant, they are parting with their money and deserve to be well served and well fed. The American businessman and restaurateur Warner Leroy summed it up pretty well when he said:

"A restaurant is a fantasy – a kind of living fantasy in which the diners are the most important members of the cast."

WARNER LEROY

I enjoy going to restaurants and it's a lovely way to celebrate a special occasion. I also love meeting a friend for a coffee in the morning in a nice coffee shop and there's something very nice about afternoon tea with china cups and saucers, and a tiered plate with sandwiches and pastries. Simple pleasures but convivial situations and worth cherishing because there is something very human and caring about sharing food with somebody and exchanging conversation and an interest in another's life. It's about making time for that other person and isn't that the essence of good relations. Here's what the comedian and violinist Henny Youngman had to say on the subject of his marriage of more than sixty years to his wife Sadie Cohen:

"Some people ask the secret of our long marriage. We take time to go to a restaurant two times a week. A little candlelight, soft music and dancing. She goes Tuesdays, I go Fridays."

HENNY YOUNGMAN

He was joking, of course.

I mentioned that The Wineport is a memorable place and the reason for that is it's the location where the RTÉ cookery programme *The Restaurant* is filmed. There's no doubt that people like cookery programmes and *The Restaurant* is hugely popular. In 2009, I was invited to take part in a cook-off against the actor Simon Delaney because both of us had previously and separately been awarded two stars for our efforts on the show. That's two out a maximum of five – and that's not good. Actually, it's the lowest score. But that was a long time ago. A time when I was less interested in food and my experience of cooking amounted to preparing meals that would be varied and healthy for my children and would pass the acid test, i.e. that they'd eat them! I don't know what Simon's excuse was.

This time was different. There was a sense of excitement from the time I arrived the night before the cook-off and was brought in the back door to a lovely room where the curtains were already drawn in case any of the diners there might see either of us and the identity of the two chefs who'd be cooking the following evening would be revealed. All very cloak and dagger, but a lot of fun and I just relaxed and enjoyed the luxury of staying overnight in a lovely hotel. I looked over my cookery notes and my menus, watched TV and chilled out. I'm glad I did because the following morning dawned bright and early with a knock on the door from the producer at seven thirty, and from then till about midnight my feet didn't hit the ground.

I have always had great admiration for the hard work that chefs do with their teams in restaurant and hotel kitchens and it was reinforced that day in Glasson. There is no truth in the rumour that 'too many cooks spoil the broth'. I was very glad of all the help the experts in that kitchen could give. There were two of us amateurs in the kitchen, wannnabe chefs, tackling our menus and looking over each other's shoulders. The craic was mighty. Simon is a very funny guy. The

work was even mightier. We were on the go the whole day, filming, testing, tasting, improving and by the time the diners arrived, we were dying to get the food out there and see and hear what they thought of our efforts, courtesy of the monitors in the kitchen and the microphones attached to the tables. It's a humbling experience, listening to people discuss the merits and otherwise of the food you have painstakingly and lovingly prepared. They show little mercy if they're not impressed. There's always the urge to just barge into the room and fight your corner. But that would ruin the whole thing.

The judges, Tom Doorley and Paolo Tullio, were joined by guest judge Paul Rankin from Belfast. The guest judge is always a bit more sympathetic than the two regulars. The corners have been well and truly knocked off them but the guest is gentler in his observations. It was a very close contest and came down to the final whistle! I won the starter course by two votes to one, Simon won the main course with a delicious lamb shank dish by two votes to one, so we're level pegging. That lamb shank was so tender, it fell off the bone and Simon served it with a load of creamy mashed potato and winter vegetables. Perfect soul food for that time of the year. None of your nouvelle cuisine in that dish. There was eatin' and drinkin' in it, and it looked so tasty. Julia Child, the American food writer, would have approved. In the film of her life with Meryl Streep in the title role, Julia made no secret of her distaste for nouvelle cuisine when she said:

"It's so beautifully arranged on the plate – you know someone's fingers have been all over it."

JULIA CHILD

Ouch, Julia! I digress and I know you're waiting with bated breath to learn the final result of the cook off between Simon Delaney and Mary Kennedy. It's one course each and time to judge the best dessert. Simon went for a coffee and banofee pie and I went for a trio of autumn berries, some poached, some made into a sorbet and some served in a cheesecake. Tom chose my dessert, Paul chose Simon's, so we are literally down to Paolo's last vote to decide the winner. And he chose ... mine. So the winner is Mary, by a whisker. We were both delighted, though, because our joint menu scored four out of a possible five points. We had certainly raised our game.

I was chuffed to have done so well and when I compared that contest to the first one and wondered what made the difference, I became convinced it was because of the different stage of life that I had reached. I have developed an interest in cooking that I didn't have before. I love feeding people, particularly my family, and though they are now grown I enjoy doing things for them when I can. When I have to leave the house very early in the morning to travel to another part of the country to film for *Nationwide*, I make a point of getting up in time to bake a batch of fairy cakes which I leave on the kitchen table, happy that when they emerge from their slumbers, the smell of freshly baked buns will waft up the stairs to them. That, of course, depends on how much longer they stay in bed. In any event, they will find those fresh buns waiting for them on the kitchen table. I also make fruit smoothies and leave them in the fridge. The idea of me baking buns and blending fruit at the crack of dawn (and sometimes before it) provides great amusement for the camera crew when we all meet up at the filming location. They're still waiting for me to bring a batch of buns with me some day. There just aren't enough hours in the day sometimes!

Leaving the buns and the smoothies for my offspring is my way of mothering them I suppose when I can't be there as they start their day. My aim is to ease their way through life and to provide comfort, love and support wherever and whenever it's needed. And if a few fairy cakes and a smoothie can bring a smile to their faces first thing in the morning, then it's no hardship to get up an hour earlier and make it happen. Like any mother I know, the welfare of my children is the first thing I think of in the morning and the last thing at night. The fact that they are grown up now and starting to make their own way in the world doesn't affect this thinking. It does give me more time to do things for myself but one part of my mind and of my heart will always be focused in their direction. There's a poem by the American poet and essayist Joaquin Miller which describes that attitude pretty well for me. He's talking about 'the bravest battle that ever was fought' and he is adamant that it was not on any battlefield or in any court room:

❧

"But deep in the walled-up woman's heart –
Of a woman that would not yield,
But bravely, silently bore her part –
Lo, there is the battlefield.
No marshalling troops, no bivouac song,
No banner to gleam and wave;
But, oh! those battles, they last so long –
From babyhood to the grave."

JOAQUIN MILLER

❧

Miller died in 1913, but the sentiments he expressed are as true for mothers today as they ever were. There are women the world over who struggle daily to provide for their children, in a way that we in the developed world can never understand. They battle against the odds and will never stint in the efforts they make for their children. I feel very privileged to have had four healthy children and I am happy to do what I can whenever and wherever I can. I treasure every minute I spend in their company, because I realise that time will diminish as life goes on and they develop other interests and take on, hopefully, the responsibility of their own families. When I must leave the house before they get up, I am more than happy to provide a little treat in the form of the fairy cakes and the smoothies. It's my pleasure and I think of them coming down and scoffing them as I drive down the motorway and on to my destination.

The nurturing aspect of my relationship with my children does centre to a sizeable extent around food. I like to make soups and leave them for them when they come in at the end of the day. They're nourishing, comforting and so simple to make. There's a Jewish proverb that comes into my head whenever I'm putting a soup together:

"Worries go down better with soup."

JEWISH PROVERB

I agree. Soup is warming, comforting and nourishing. The very act of eating a soup with a spoon from a bowl slows you down and has a calming, relaxing effect. I'm a great believer in soup and, of course, in bread for dipping!

My four children and I like to go to restaurants together and with the cousins, and we have fairly catholic tastes. Italian goes down a treat, is good value and you get a reasonable bang for your buck, especially when you're trying to fill growing men with hollow legs. As the Australian comedian George Miller said:

"The trouble with eating Italian food is that five or six days later you're hungry again."

George Miller

Thank goodness for that! It's satisfying, tasty and hits the spot for the hungry young men in my life. We also like to stay at home, particularly on a Friday, and order in. Sometimes Chinese, sometimes Indian, always perfect for an easy night watching TV or a DVD. Every time we eat a Chinese takeaway though, somebody brings up Miss Piggy's immortal line years ago on *The Muppet Show* when she was offered chopsticks in a Chinese restaurant. She looked at the waiter, flicked her hair back and in her poshest Miss Piggy voice entoned:

"You don't sew with a fork, so I see no reason to eat with knitting needles."

MISS PIGGY

No flies on Miss Piggy. When that memory of their childhood days watching *The Muppet Show* is recalled, we tuck in to a good old feast of informal and relaxed eating by the fire.

There's no doubt that sharing food with other people is one of life's great pleasures. The American writer Ambrose Bierce defines the verb 'to dine' as:

"To eat a good dinner in good company, and eat it slow."

AMBROSE BIERCE

ꝸ

I appreciate that pleasure now in a way I didn't when I was younger. I was one of those people who was always conscious of my weight. I was an advertiser's dream, constantly aspiring to be a different shape to the one I was. I was never happy with my weight, even though I was fit and healthy and played sport and was always running. I never remember a time when I was happy with the way I looked. I was always on, or going on, a diet, although I never ever stuck to them. Every Monday, I would wake full of good intentions. I would eat only what was good and healthy. That resolve would last till I got hungry, which was about lunchtime. I was a classic example of the maxim that: 'The second day of a diet is always easier than the first. By the second day, you're off it.'

That was me. What a waste of energy, and what a stupid way to spend your youth. My mother was always watching me to see what I was eating. She was worried, naturally, that I might develop an eating disorder. I was typical of lots of young girls who were being bombarded with Twiggy and Mary Quant and the stick-insect look so much a feature of models to this day. The sad thing is that when I look back at photographs taken at the times when I remember feeling unhappy about my body shape, I realise now that my body shape was fine, I was healthy, not fat, slim in fact. I could have saved myself a lot of angst and enjoyed food more. There's a funny saying about dieting that is actually quite sad when you think about it:

"Blessed are those who hunger and thirst,
for they are sticking to their diets."

With the wisdom of middle age, I can see that it is the height of nonsense to be living life that way, especially when we consider the number of people all around the world who are hungry and thirsty for reasons of poverty, famine and war. I believe we have a duty as parents in this part of the world to educate our children in good nutrition and to have a healthy respect for good eating habits and exercise, and to eliminate the diet mentality from our lives. There are lots of people who overeat and eat the wrong things, in the wrong quantities, without adequate exercise to burn off the calories. They convince themselves they'll start a diet next Monday and all will be well. All will not be well. Bad eating habits are difficult to overcome. Diets are difficult to adhere to, particularly as we get older. Nancy Casurella, a doctor from Arizona, offers a word of caution here:

"The older we get, the tougher it is to lose weight because, by then, your body and your fat are really good friends."

NANCY CASURELLA

That's for sure. The other home truth is that, as we get older, it's nice to have a bit of a shape. It's nice to be fit and healthy and to enjoy food and exercise and good company. I regret all the years I spent striving to be different to the way I was. I wish I could have enjoyed that time without constantly worrying about what I was, or wasn't, eating. What a waste of time, energy and lovely food!

Thankfully, I've reached this stage in life intact. I realise there are many people who started off like me, overly conscious of food and dieting, but who, unlike me, did

succumb to eating disorders and all the heartache and ill health that go with them. Whether you're of the mentality that views food as merely fuel to keep hunger at bay or views food as a sociable and pleasurable experience, it's important I think to appreciate and respect the part that food plays in our lives. I fall, belatedly, into the second category and I enjoy the cooking and the sharing of food. I really do wish though that I'd got to this stage earlier in life. Think of all the occasions I could have enjoyed without the feeling of guilt that I was eating creamy sauces perhaps or cakes or biscuits. There were times when I would throw caution to the wind and eat whatever goodies were on offer, but I would always be thinking to the next day when I would make amends and be very careful about what I'd eat. The very notion of 'making amends' underlines the feeling of guilt that accompanied eating certain lovely foods. What a shame.

The consolation is that I have finally overcome that guilt and enjoy the food, the wine, the company and the circumstance. At long last! I think it's fitting to finish this chapter with reference both to food and the day on which it was written, St Valentine's Day:

"Forget love, I'd rather fall in chocolate!"

Community Spirit

"As 2010 draws to a close
The Emly story must be told.
Another year of great success
With medals, trophies and all the rest."

DENIS HEFFERNAN

Those are the opening lines of a series of verses penned by Denis Heffernan, a man whose name is synonymous with the Tidy Towns initiative in the tiny village of Emly in County Tipperary. I was delighted to receive the poem through the post to the *Nationwide* office in Cork and it was a further example of the pride Denis and the people of Emly have in their home place. I first came across this energetic man, his daughter Sharon who is the chairperson of Emly Tidy Towns committee, and all the hardworking volunteers when they travelled to Dublin Castle in early September 2009 to learn their fate in that year's competition, and when it was announced that their village was the overall winner for the year, St Patrick's Hall was the scene of unbridled euphoria. It seemed as if the whole of Emly had travelled to Dublin and they were all rushing up on stage, Denis waving his walking stick in the air as he led the rest in a few bars of the Tipperary anthem 'Slievenamon':

"Alone, all alone, by the wave-washed strand
And alone in a crowded hall.
The hall it is gay and the waves they are grand
But my heart is not here at all."

CHARLES J. KICKHAM

It was certainly a crowded hall, it was gay and I do believe that the heart of everyone of those Emly residents was dying to get back to their little corner of west Tipperary, to bring the trophy back and display it proudly, a testament to their hard work. It's also a testament to the power of community spirit and volunteerism which can give great heart and purpose to a community and be an essential part of individual and collective well being. Cicero put it very succinctly nearly two thousand years ago and what he said is as true today as it was then:

"We were born to unite with our fellow men, and to join in community with the human race."

CICERO

❧

The people of Emly have certainly united over the years in their efforts to take on the big guns in the Tidy Towns, and I know from a visit to the village last year that their effort has also led to a most welcoming and friendly group of people who radiate good humour and energy, concern for their home place and for each other.

❧

"Is ar scáth a chéile a mhaireann na daoine."

(*"People live in each other's shadows."*)

IRISH PROVERB

❧

When President McAleese visited Emly to unveil the plaque commemorating the 2009 Tidy Towns win, *Nationwide* was on hand to record the occasion. I arrived in the sun-soaked village early on a Saturday morning and was struck by the atmosphere of joy that radiated everywhere. The place was spick and span. There wasn't a blade of grass out of place. Leaves had been swept up at first light. We're talking here about the leaves that had fallen overnight because the streets had also been vigorously swept last thing on Friday evening. There was bunting hanging from the lampposts. No marks for guessing the colours of that bunting in the Premier County! Even the hanging baskets had blue and yellow pansies. The streets were a riot of colour, from the window frames and front doors of the houses to the benches and the barrels along the way. Emly was *en fête*, and full of happiness and laughter. It had certainly taken to heart the words of Pope John Paul II when he advised:

"A community needs a soul if it is to become
a true home for human beings.
You, the people, give it this soul."

POPE JOHN PAUL II

There was no doubting the soul of that community. It was evident in all aspects of the village, including the hospitality of the people. When I got out of my car,

Denis Heffernan was there with his hand outstretched in greeting. I was whisked to Jonas and Betty Callanan's pub and restaurant, where there was a wonderful display of sandwiches, scones and big pots of tea to be enjoyed by all and sundry on this day of days. Denis was very happy and very proud that this day had arrived. And he had every right to be. It was he who got the Tidy Towns committee up and running in 1987 and gathered a group of willing volunteers from different groups in the village, the school, the clubs, the church. That's some achievement in a village with a population of about eight hundred people. All age groups rowed in and Denis passed the mantle of chairperson of the committee to his daughter Sharon in 2005. I was very impressed with all that had been achieved over the years in this small community. There's the Emigrant Wall in the village commemorating all of the local people who had left in search of a better life. Although there are fewer than a thousand people living in Emly now, it boasted a population of four thousand, four hundred inhabitants in 1841. The Tidy Towns committee have also set up a Heritage Trail, they take great pride in their bio diversity programme, and, at the top of the town behind the church is the Four Seasons Park, open to the public and full of colour, scent and texture in its abundant growth. A very comprehensive amount of improvement undertaken in a small community for sure, but as the anthropologist Margaret Mead said:

❦

"Never doubt that a small group of thoughtful committed citizens can change the world. Indeed, it is the only thing that ever has."

MARGARET MEAD

❦

At eleven o'clock in the morning, as the combined bands were playing 'Slievenamon', the president's car pulled up at the podium constructed outside the church gates and the excitement and happiness were every bit as palpable as they had been in Dublin Castle when Emly's name came out of the gold envelope.

❦

"Then there was the president who came
to see our town
Oh what a day that was,
the sun was shining down.
Eoin Ryan and Mary K from RTÉ came down
And every place was lovely
and I felt so very proud."

DENIS HEFFERNAN

I have no doubt that Denis' pride was repeated in the heart of every other person in Emly on that Saturday morning. It was a reason to be proud of community living at its best in this country. Unfortunately, that sense of community is not repeated in all parts, and was certainly in short supply during the years of the Celtic Tiger when many people seemed preoccupied with their individual lives and attainments and less so with the general and common good.

"Community is as endangered by surplus as it is by deficit. If there is too much money floating around it enables people to have no need of each other."

BILL MCKIBBEN

Those are the words of the American environmentalist Bill McKibben and the evidence exists that, in these recessionary times, people seem to be looking again at what's important and worthwhile in life and taking stock of their neighbours and their communities. It didn't take a recession though for that mentality to sweep through Emly. It feels as if it has always been there. The camaraderie and neighbourliness that was evident in Emly on that Saturday morning would gladden your heart and lift your spirits. I got the impression that people look out for each other there, that they care about what's happening in each other's lives and that they would offer a helping hand in difficult circumstances just as they were prepared to do in the circumstances of unbridled joy as they celebrated the first visit of a president to their village.

❧

> *"Unselfish and noble actions are the most radiant pages in the biography of souls."*
>
> HENRY DAVID THOREAU

❧

There were many examples of unselfish and noble actions in Emly that day as its inhabitants emerged from their houses with trays of sandwiches and with chairs to place in front of the podium. They were there to celebrate the culmination of more than twenty years of striving for success, and we all know that success demands sacrifice and a lot of hard work. Obviously, the people of Emly were willing to oblige with many hours of noble hard work in preparation for the judging in the Tidy Towns. They give the impression that they enjoy the legacy they are creating to enrich the life of their community today and for generations to come. They illustrate for me the truth of that Greek proverb which I love for its simplicity and subtlety:

ᘓ

"A civilisation flourishes when people plant trees under which they will never sit."

GREEK PROVERB

ᘓ

I enjoyed my day filming for *Nationwide* on the day of the presidential visit to Emly in Tipperary. The sun shone, the birds sang, the bands played, the flowers bloomed and, most importantly, the people laughed and exuded pride of place grown from community spirit. I felt proud of my countrymen and women in that corner of west Tipperary on the Limerick border, and I was very conscious of that unique quality that sets us apart from other peoples in other countries, that sense of responsibility to the community in which we live and the people who share it with us. George Bernard Shaw felt that responsibility in his day and described it very eloquently and very clearly when he wrote:

"I am of the opinion that my life belongs to the whole community and as long as I live, it is my privilege to do for it whatever I can. I want to be thoroughly used up when I die, for the harder I work, the more I live."

GEORGE BERNARD SHAW

Community spirit is, of course, stronger in some places than in others. There's a positive energy and a passion that is infectious and seductive in places like Emly. It would make you want to bottle those qualities and bring them to other areas that have not been blessed with a deep sense of community. When I was growing up in Clondalkin, the community spirit was strong and the village had great soul and heart. It was full of people who gave of their free time tirelessly and willingly to develop areas of interest in that fledgling community. My father was a founder member of the Credit Union. He was also involved with the Parish Planned Giving – going door to door collecting the weekly donations for the upkeep of the parish – the Swimming Pool committee, Muintir na Tíre and the St Vincent de Paul Society. My mother was a member of the ICA, Gael Linn, the church choir and the church cleaning group. And they weren't unique or unusual. Many of their friends and neighbours were involved in parish activities too. As the writer and spiritual director Elizabeth Andrew says:

"Volunteers do not necessarily have the time; they just have the heart."

ELIZABETH ANDREW

They had the heart and they brought heart and soul to their corner of the universe and their children benefited greatly from their efforts. It's more difficult nowadays to engender that sense of volunteerism in people who are working hard to pay a hefty mortgage along with other bills and to educate their children, but in places like Emly, where that quality is present, there's great joy and wholesome living to be found.

Another great example of community spirit can be found in Tralee in the late summer during the world-renowned festival, the highlight of which is, of course, the contest to find the Rose of Tralee. In fact, that spirit is present right through the year because the committees and the volunteers embark on their planning and organising almost as soon as the Rose is crowned and sets off on her year of engagements representing Kerry and the festival in places all around the world where members of the Irish diaspora have settled.

I've been involved with the festival in different ways over the years, beginning in 1996 when I was asked to travel to Brussels to present the Belgian Rose Selection Ball. I have to say I was pleasantly surprised by the strength of feeling among the Irish community in that city. The selection took place in a Belgian setting but you could just as easily have been in a hotel in the heart of Ireland for the banter, the accents, the Irishness of the people present. It's true that 'the savage loves his native shore' and it's also true that when you leave that shore and live abroad, you appreciate your heritage for the way it sets you apart from others. There was a great sense of camaraderie and belonging among the people gathered that evening in Brussels. There was great joy and pride in their shared homeland, not unlike that which I witnessed in Emly some fourteen years later. They chatted together, getting to know fellow countrymen and women who had come from all parts for the selection. They cheered on the contestants and they sang with gusto:

"The pale moon was rising above the green
mountains,
The sun was declining beneath the blue sea;
When I strayed with my love by the pure crystal
fountain,
That stands in the beautiful vale of Tralee."

William Pembroke Mulchinock

That was my first direct involvement with the Rose of Tralee. I had, of course, grown up watching the contest on television. It was a highlight of our summer viewing, something to look forward to as the evenings were closing in and the new school year beckoned. All my family watched it, with different agendas undoubtedly. I never asked, but I'm sure my brothers were admiring the contestants. My parents enjoyed it all too, picking out the winner. My mother had a notion that Limerick had the most beautiful young girls in the country. This point always seemed to be part of the conversation during the Rose of Tralee and all through the year, she used to cut out pictures from the newspapers of Limerick girls at various functions to prove her point. For my part, I loved the style but, more particularly, I was mesmerised by the accomplishments of these young women who were only a few years older than me.

That admiration has been reinforced over the past few years during my involvement with the contest. As a judge I have got to know the Roses well, and they are Irish women to be proud of. They are intelligent, hard working, caring, funny and friendly, and their parents must be so proud watching them on stage in the Dome. Having spent a number of days with them, we judges feel very proud of them too. Sitting in the front row watching them chatting and perhaps performing a party piece, I feel nervous for them all and want them to do well. It brings me right back to when my children were small and I was sitting in the audience at the Feis Maitiú, watching them perform their poem, willing them to do well, reciting every word with them in my head and hoping they wouldn't stumble over a verse and lose their nerve. It's exactly the same in the Dome. And the words of the song could have been written for any of them:

"She was lovely and fair as the rose of the summer.
Yet 'twas not her beauty alone that won me;
Oh no, 'twas the truth in her eye ever dawning,
That made me love Mary, the Rose of Tralee."

WILLIAM PEMBROKE MULCHINOCK

The song was written for a young Tralee girl and you'd have to look long and hard to come across a more romantic story than that of Mary O'Connor and William Pembroke Mulchinock. Mary was one of four children living with her parents in a little thatched cabin in Brogue Lane in Tralee. They were a poor family. Her father was a cobbler, as were most of the inhabitants of the lane and her mother was a dairymaid. Mary followed in her mother's footsteps and went to work as a maid for the Mulchinocks, a wealthy merchant family who had a woollen and linen drapery shop. They lived in a big house in West Villa and around the time Mary joined their domestic staff, the father died and his widow Margaret was living in the house with her three sons William Pembroke, Edward and Henry and her married daughter Maria who had two small children, Margaret and Anne.

Now you probably think you could write the rest of the story with William falling for the peasant girl Mary, who had grown into a stunningly beautiful young woman with dark hair and huge eyes. Yes and no! That is true but it's only the start of a most romantic and tragically sad story. I know you're dying to find out what happened, so I will delay no longer. Mary was an intelligent girl and she was taken from the kitchen staff and promoted to the position of children's maid for young Margaret and Anne. William was always a bit of a dreamer and a romantic soul. When his brother Henry died young, he expressed his sorrow in verse:

ᘔ

"For him of the fair young brow I weep,
Who takes in the churchyard now his sleep;
For he was the star above Sun-bright,
That tinged with the light of love my night."

William Pembroke Mulchinock

ᘔ

Anyway, William spotted Mary in his sister's house, fell in love with her, even though he and she knew the liaison would be frowned upon, not only because she was from Brogue Lane and he from West Villa but because she was a poor papist and he was an upstanding member of the Established Church. In spite of this, they started seeing each other and William was a frequent visitor to Mary's home in Brogue Lane. He proposed marriage several times but she declined because she knew it would be the end of his grand life, and that he would 'rue the day' he met her. Finally, she acquiesced and said she'd give him her answer the following day when they'd meet at the Daniel O'Connell rally in the town.

There was a fracas the following day in Denny Street; a man was injured and subsequently died, and William Mulchinock was falsely accused. The thinking was that his influential family would stop at nothing to keep himself and Mary apart. He fled the country, for fear of being arrested, assuring Mary he would return to marry her when matters cooled down. He ended up in India and became a war correspondent there. He finally made his way back to Ireland, determined to seek out and marry Mary. The country was in the throes of the Great Famine by that stage and as he arrived into Tralee a funeral was making its way through the town. It was Mary who had died. William was beside himself with grief. He subsequently married a girl from Ballinasloe, went to America with her and had two children before they separated and he returned to Tralee unable to forget his first love. William sought solace from his heartbreak in drink and he died in 1864, at the age of forty-four. His last wish was to be buried alongside Mary. This wish was granted. William Pembroke Mulchinock and Mary O'Connor are buried side by side in the graveyard at Clogherbrien. Before his death of a broken heart, William penned a further stanza to his song in honour of his beloved Mary:

"In the far fields of India, mid war's dreadful thunders,
Her voice was a solace and comfort to me,
But the chill hand of death has now rent us asunder,
I'm lonely tonight for the Rose of Tralee."

William Pembroke Mulchinock

Wouldn't that melt the heart of a stone? I did tell you it was a very romantic story and a very sad one at that. In 2009, to celebrate the fiftieth anniversary of the Rose of Tralee contest, a statue of William and Mary was unveiled in the Rose Garden in Tralee, a reminder of the story of the very first Rose of Tralee and also a tribute to the success of the contest, which is the centrepiece of the Festival of Kerry and therefore a tribute to the hard work and spirit of the people who organise it every year.

There is an army of volunteers who come together for the festival. Some of them take their annual leave from work and dedicate themselves to the smooth running of this international event which showcases the very best of family fun and community spirit. The Rose of Tralee is something that is unique to Ireland, something that sets us apart from other countries and cultures. It's a celebration of accomplished, confident and caring young Irish women from all parts of the world. They come back to their ancestral home and show great pride in their roots. There is a carnival atmosphere in the Dome during the televised programmes, with banners and flags and hats and hooters. Those two nights are the culmination of a mammoth organisational and multifaceted initiative with many highlights, including the spectacular Rose Parade through the town on Saturday evening, during which the different Roses are introduced to the crowds who come out in their thousands to cheer and to welcome the visitors. The Escorts are always attentive and well behaved towards the Roses and their families. A feature of the festival that really appeals to me is the sight of young girls from the town and beyond who gather outside the hotel waiting for the Roses to emerge. They carry copybooks into which they have stuck pictures of the Roses representing the different Irish centres and the idea is to get the autograph of each Rose beside her photograph. Isn't that a lovely idea? Of course, all of the Roses oblige. That's a tradition you'd be hard pressed to find in any other part of the world. It allows an interaction between the young autograph hunters and these radiant young women who provide a good role model for these youngsters as they prepare to enter their teenage years.

Staging all the different aspects of the Rose of Tralee each year is a huge undertaking on the part of the organising committee and that army of volunteers. There are mentors or chaperones for the Roses, their families, the Escorts, the judges. There are liaison teams for the press and television crews. There is somebody to help out at every turn. They all work together as a team, often very late into the night and they never ever complain or get cranky. They have great pride in this festival and in their home place of Tralee. Just like the people of Emly. Such people make me very proud to be Irish and to be associated with them. They have an infectious good humour and an attitude of can do. They give credence to the thinking of Edward Everett Hale:

"I am only one, but I am one. I cannot do everything, but I can do something. And I will not let what I cannot do interfere with what I can do."

EDWARD EVERETT HALE

Hale was a child prodigy who enrolled at Harvard University at the age of thirteen and graduated second in his class. I think it's a safe bet to presume, therefore, that his positive thinking stood him in good stead! That positive attitude is very evident among the people involved in the Festival of Kerry and the Rose of Tralee. They are community spirit in action and we are all beneficiaries of that spirit.

"Give fools their gold and knaves their power;
let fortune's bubbles rise and fall;
who sows a field, or trains a flower,
or plants a tree is more than all."

JOHN GREENLEAF WHITTIER

Those lines from the pen of the nineteenth-century Massachusetts poet John Greenleaf Whittier throw a light on another aspect of living that is central to our national identity and that has shaped us as a people and a community. I grew up in suburban Dublin, of parents who grew up in inner-city Dublin. I have no relatives who are farmers, but I admire greatly and value deeply the way life is lived in the non-urban parts of our country. I know I will be accused of being naïve and old fashioned. I know it is well nigh impossible to make a living from farming alone these days, that most farming households have to diversify and have one partner working off the farm. I know that city folk feel farmers have it easy and they complain a lot. But I also know that in rural Ireland, there is great community spirit. Farmers helping each other out at different times of the year, supporting events in their villages and towns, looking out for older people and for those who have fallen on hard times perhaps. Those people who sow fields tend to be open minded and open hearted. They have time for a chat, a cup of tea. As Ruth Stout, the American writer who became known as the 'No Dig Duchess' for her policy of year-round mulching and trouble-free farming, put it:

"Farmers are philosophical.
They have learned that it is less wearing
to shrug than to beat their breasts."

RUTH STOUT

That friendly, easy-going attitude is a joy and it is to be seen and felt in abundance at the National Ploughing Championships, which we look forward to featuring on *Nationwide* every year and which last September celebrated its eightieth anniversary. The championships take place over three days. The venue is provided by a farmer and the carnival rolls into town. It's a mammoth undertaking, with miles of all-weather trackways laid down, tents for the thousands of agribusiness and other exhibitors, outdoor areas for the machinery displays, furrows for the ploughing competitions, some by teams of horses ploughing in the traditional manner, some by state-of-the-art tractors. There are lots of food stalls and attractions, music stages, fashion shows. The event is a well-oiled machine (if you'll pardon the pun) and it's well oiled, once again, by the army of volunteers who offer their services and give of their time so that this celebration of a truly central part of our identity runs smoothly.

The numbers of people who attend each year are staggering. On day one in 2010, for instance, the attendance, at 66,000, showed an increase of 20,000 on the opening day for the previous year. They come from all parts of the country, families on a day out, groups of farmers studying the latest findings and machinery, school tours, youngsters eyeing up the opposite sex. The common denominator between all of the people who attend is their good humour, their down-to-earth demeanour and their wellies. Some of these wellies are sensible and functional. They're usually the ones worn by the men. There's nothing down-to-earth though about the wellies worn by the women. They come in all colours and patterns and, each year, there seems to be a new style, and an accompanying new style of trousers to show the wellies off to their best advantage. It's a great day out and an important one too, bringing up to €10 million into the local economy. There's an easygoing unhurried air to the day as you stroll around the Ploughing Championships, which reflects nicely, I think, the easygoing and unhurried lifestyle that I have witnessed among the farming community in our country. After all:

"Life on a farm is a school of patience;
You can't hurry the crops or make
an ox in two days."

ALAIN FOURNIER

I agree with what Alain Fournier, the French writer and soldier who died in the First World War, says there. The nature of farming and living on the land gives a certain quality to the people who live by its rhythms. They have time for people, they open their homes and their hearts without any fuss, and they have a deep sense of the community of which they are a part. These qualities are manifest in the volunteers who turn up year after year to help out at the Ploughing Championships. You meet them at every step of the way. They direct you to the Park and Ride facility. You leave your car and climb up on a trailer hitched to a tractor, provided by a local farmer. You're driven to the entrance, manned by volunteers. There are people to show you around if you're lost. I have sampled the most delicious fruit cake, made by local women for the people who are working at the championships. I have been given lifts to various parts of the site to interview a participant by local volunteers, in jeeps provided for the three days of this huge event. The volunteers work hard, but they love it. When I watch them looking out for people to assist or jobs to do, I always think of the words of Mother Teresa who dedicated her life to the people she described as 'the poorest of the poor' in Calcutta:

"Unless a life is lived for others, it is not worthwhile."

MOTHER TERESA

The people who volunteer in this country have families, jobs, worries, joys. They also have a sense of responsibility to their community and a big heart. Whether they're volunteering their time for the Tidy Towns, the Rose of

Tralee, the Ploughing Championships, or any one of the many events and activities that happen up and down the country, their time and work are precious and valuable. They make things happen. Another example, known to us all, is the GAA, distinctly Irish, hugely successful and run by volunteers. My own children have all, at some stage, benefited from their involvement in the GAA, playing when they were younger, and after that, for two of them, their involvement continued with Lucy coaching little ones on Saturday mornings in Ballyboden St Enda's, and Tom still volunteering as a *maor* in Croke Park. It's a wonderful organisation, active in every corner of the country and incredibly supportive of the communities in which it operates.

For a touching example of that support, we need look no further than the way in which the GAA family came together to offer assistance at the time of the funeral of Michaela McAreavey in January of this year. It was a horrifically sad time for her family and friends and, true to form, the GAA turned out in force to facilitate people coming to pay their respects and to form a guard of honour on Michaela's final journey. I hope that show of love and support provided some consolation to her grieving family. Ar dheis Dé go raibh a hanam óg, uasal.

I have travelled to a fair number of countries over the years, and I can safely say that I have never come across anything like that level of voluntary service in any other nation in the world. Volunteering in the community is something that we should be very proud of as Irish people. Our volunteers are an example to us all, and I know from the people I have met in places like Emly, Tralee and at the Ploughing that they go home at the end of the event invigorated, exhausted and, most importantly, happy in the knowledge that they have played a part in the success of something that has benefitted their community and enhanced the quality of life of its people. A job well done. After talk of the Ploughing Championships and in honour of their eighty years in existence, I think it would be appropriate to finish this chapter with a farming idiom. It's from a poem I learned in school and which I like to quote at the end of a long day of hard but satisfying work. It's from Gray's 'Elegy Written in a Country Churchyard':

❧

"The curfew tolls the knell of parting day,
The lowing herd wind slowly o'er the lea;
The ploughman homeward plods his weary way,
And leaves the world to darkness and to me."

THOMAS GRAY

Out in Africa

"Africa, my Africa;
Africa, my motherland.
Land of milk and honey,
land of natural beauty,
a land where I live."

Abisoye Sejoro

❦

The poem 'Africa', written by young Nigerian poet Abisoye Sejoro, paints a picture that simply and accurately describes for me the Africa that I have visited on several occasions over the past nine years. I've travelled to different countries for different reasons. I made a DVD for GOAL in Uganda. I visited agricultural projects in Eritrea and Ethiopia with the Irish Farmer's Association charity Self Help. I taught self-awareness to primary-school children through the medium of sport and games with Playing for Life, founded by Tracy Piggott. That took me to Malawi and Tanzania. I wrote about my visit to Kenya in *Lines I Love* and I have travelled to Liberia and to Chad to record programmes for *Nationwide*. While those countries have their different traditions and different difficulties, they are all places of breathtaking beauty, they have very valuable natural resources, and they are home to people who are intensely proud of their heritage and their motherland. They are also places of great poverty and, in some cases, great unrest, injustice and corruption.

Liberia is a case in point. The 2005 Christmas edition of *Nationwide* came from the capital Monrovia, from the Irish Defence Forces camp that formed part of the United Nations Mission in Liberia (UNMIL). This was established following the second civil war in the country, which began in 1999 and culminated in the flight of the president Charles Taylor to Nigeria in 2003. In 1989, Taylor had returned to his native country from Libya, where he had trained as a guerrilla fighter. On his return, he set up the National Patriotic Front of Liberia in opposition to the president Samuel Doe. The first civil war ensued and in the heel of the hunt, Taylor, who had a reputation as a dangerous warlord, was elected president in 1997. His campaign slogan is telling:

"He killed my ma, he killed my pa,
but I will vote for him."

Fear was his weapon of choice during his electoral campaign and during his presidency. He established questionable relationships with neighbouring Sierra Leone and is credited with providing that country with arms in exchange for blood diamonds. The wealth went into his own coffers and the people remained poor and afraid. This country whose name, ironically, derives from the word 'liberation', is bordered by West Guinea and Ivory Coast as well as by Sierra Leone to the west and the Atlantic Ocean to the south. It has a population of three and a half million people, hundreds of thousands of whom were killed during the first and second civil wars.

I don't think it's an exaggeration to say that Charles Taylor brought Liberia to its knees. When our plane landed in Monrovia in early December 2005, two years after his departure, we touched down in total darkness. There was no electricity in the country. We travelled in an army jeep to the headquarters of the Irish peacekeepers. The only light was from the headlights of the vehicle. There was no moon that night, so we could see absolutely nothing. That changed when we arrived at Camp Clara, named for the County Offaly home place of its first commanding officer. A generator provided electricity in the camp that housed the Irish and the Swedish battalions of this UN peacekeeping force. The irony that it was formerly the Hotel Africa, favoured by Charles Taylor to entertain his guests, including warlords from neighbouring countries, was not lost on us. There was a central hotel building and several thatched circular holiday bungalows that led down to a beach. I'd mention two things here: the main building and the cottages were riddled with bullet holes and debris, and the water was totally contaminated to the extent that, even though the heat and humidity were oppressive, swimming was out of the question. That was a bit of a disappointment for us during our four-day filming sojourn. Can you imagine what it was like for the soldiers in full uniform not to be able to cool off in the water that was literally lapping all around their camp? There's a sentence that has always struck a chord with me from the book *Desert Solitaire: A Season in the Wilderness*, written by the American essayist and environmentalist, Edward Abbey.

"When a man must be afraid to drink freely
from his country's rivers and streams,
that country is no longer fit to live in."

EDWARD ABBEY

Never mind drinking the water in Monrovia – to swim in it would be asking for trouble! And, yes, at the end of 2005, that country seemed to me to be unfit to live in. When day broke and we went filming with the Irish peacekeepers, our eyes were opened to the abject poverty and the wholesale destruction of the city by Charles Taylor and his cohorts. The bridge over the Mesurado river, linking UN headquarters with the road into the city centre, was full of bullet and rocket holes. The roads were dirt tracks. Randall Street, the country's main thoroughfare, is about the same length and width as Dublin's O'Connell Street. It could take anything up to an hour to drive from one end of it to the other so packed was it with people sitting on the ground, selling and buying a myriad of produce, including dried and fresh fish, chicken feet, various hooves, their few vegetables and other items. Electricity wasn't the only commodity denied to these people. There were no schools open, though there was a police force being trained by UNMIL. There was also no transport system. One of Charles Taylor's parting shots had been to sell the entire rail system to a Chinese interest for $2 million. The buyer paid over the money, lifted the railway, track by track and removed it from the country.

There's a high incidence of HIV/AIDS in Liberia, as in other African countries, and we visited a hospice for the dying run by Mother Teresa's Missionaries of Charity, which has been adopted by the Irish peacekeepers as one of their charities in Liberia. There's not a lot to do when you're off duty in a place like Monrovia and the Irish troops divided their spare time between this hospice and an orphanage for children whose parents had been killed during the civil war. You'd be very proud of our defence forces in a situation like this, and their charitable commitments were all the more obvious when seen side by side with the leisure-time pursuits of their colleagues at Hotel Africa. The Swedish troops seemed to spend all of their free time in the gym, or running, or watching DVDs. Nothing whatsoever wrong with that, but the Irish tradition of volunteerism and charity work was alive and well among the young men and women in Camp Clara. Although they may not have realised it at the time, they had taken on board the words of Mother Teresa by volunteering at the hospice run by her nuns and also by volunteering at the orphanage run by two young adult brothers, orphans themselves:

"We must use time wisely and forever realise that the time is always ripe to do right."

MOTHER TERESA

The first thing I noticed when we arrived at the hospice for the dying was the enormous metal gate, which was bolted shut. A hospital set-up, with the promise of food and medicines, would be very attractive to thieves, particularly when those thieves are impoverished to the extent that they would be insensitive to the needs of the patients inside. A way had to be cleared for us to get through the gate, such was the crowd of men, women and children camped outside. In my naiveté, I thought they were waiting to visit their relatives. No. They were waiting for leftover food to be handed out through the gate so that they could feed their families.

The contrast between the commotion outside the hospice and the silence inside was chilling. The only noise was the crying of sick, emaciated babies. The adults were sick and emaciated too, but they didn't make any noise at all, they just lay on their beds with a sheet over them, waiting to die. The stench of death was in the air but so also was the sense of love and care that was being provided to the skeletal figures by the diminutive sisters in their blue-trimmed white saris and also by the young Irish men and women in their army uniforms. These off-duty peacekeepers washed, fed and played with the HIV infected children and babies. They sat with the adults, holding a hand perhaps or mopping a brow, letting them know that they were not alone as they prepared to move on from this world and the awful suffering associated with it.

HIV/AIDS is raging through the continent of Africa. A child is orphaned every fifteen seconds as a result of its carnage. Antiretroviral drugs are available but access to them is so often the problem. Education is key, and the de-stigmatisation of the disease. The responsibility lies with us all. As our own Bono said:

"History will judge us on how we respond
to the AIDS emergency in Africa …
whether we stood around with watering cans
and watched while a whole continent
burst into flames … or not."

BONO

Heads of state will continue to negotiate a solution to this problem. I'm proud of the fact that they have people like Bono and Bob Geldof keeping HIV/AIDS on the world agenda. Those boys will keep the world leaders on their toes. And while that argument continues and hopefully progresses, I'm proud as punch of people like those Irish peacekeepers in Liberia who gave of their free time to alleviate the isolation and suffering of those unfortunate people in the hospice for the dying in Monrovia.

I also visited the orphanage for children whose parents had been killed during the civil war and saw the wonderful work the Irish troops were doing there too. As I said, it's run by two young adult men, brothers orphaned in the same circumstances, who rounded up children who had literally been left with nowhere to go. The orphanage is very basic. In fact, the young boys were sleeping in a dormitory with a big gap in the side wall. The reason for this was the fact that it was actually not a real wall at all but a termite hill which had softened and caved in. The Irish troops were in the process of building a block structure – a shed to you and me; a brand-new dormitory to the young boys in the orphanage. They provided the blocks, the building materials and the labour and while they were there, they played football with the children. All in their free time. I thought I'd burst with pride watching them interact with the children. They have made such a difference to those young lives. They are a living example of another pronouncement of Mother Teresa:

"Let no one ever come to you without leaving better and happier. Be the living expression of God's kindness in your face, kindness in your eyes, kindness in your smile."

MOTHER TERESA

❧

There is no doubt that Liberia was a broken country after the reign of Charles Taylor. Elections had been held in November, a few weeks before the *Nationwide* team visit, and on 16 January 2006 a woman, Ellen Johnson Sirleaf, was inaugurated President of Liberia. Conditions are improving slowly for the people. Johnson Sirleaf has prioritised women's rights and education and the rebuilding of post-conflict Liberia. There are still major obstacles to be overcome in a country half of whose population survive on less than a dollar a day and where 65 per cent of the population is illiterate. There is hope though. Compulsory elementary education has been introduced and while there is still a huge proportion of children who work at stalls instead of sitting in classrooms, nobody doubts that education is the only sure way forward. As Nelson Mandela himself said:

❧

"Education is the most powerful weapon which you can use to change the world."

NELSON MANDELA

ℵ

As if to illustrate this point, United Nations research has shown that educating young girls has a greater impact on their health than nutrition, safe drinking water and sanitation. Liberians seem to have confidence in their twenty-fourth president, the first woman president on the continent of Africa. There's a Liberian proverb that says:

ℵ

"If the townspeople are happy, look for the chief."

LIBERIAN PROVERB

ℵ

The people of Liberia are struggling still in the aftermath of civil war. Seventy-five per cent of the population is unemployed. But the country's infrastructure is being rebuilt. President Sirleaf has overseen the construction of 800 miles of roadway, there is some electricity but, even today, only one in every ten people has access to electricity. A mere one third of the people in Liberia have access to clean drinking water and less than a quarter to sanitary facilities. They're not being attacked though. Their sons, some as young as nine years of age, are not being kidnapped, drugged and trained as child soldiers and proclaiming that:

"Guns were our mothers and fathers.
They protected us, they got us food."

Charles Taylor was eventually extradited from Nigeria and was accompanied by Irish troops, members of UNMIL, to Sierra Leone. He was subsequently transferred to a UN detention centre in The Hague and is standing trial for crimes against humanity. The Irish Defence Forces have moved on from Liberia to other places in need of protection, places like Chad, for instance, where *Nationwide* recorded a programme to mark St Patrick's Day. I have no doubt the Irish troops are greatly missed by the people whose lives they touched during their tour of duty in Monrovia. Liberia's loss was Chad's gain.

I began this chapter by mentioning the characteristics that the African countries I have visited share. Poverty is certainly a common denominator. They also have beautiful landscapes, awe-inspiring scenery. Tanzania, for instance, although largely agricultural, depends quite strongly on a developing tourist industry that is centred around its natural beauty. The majesty of Mount Kilimanjaro, the highest mountain in Africa, is well documented. Its height, at almost twenty thousand feet, has given rise to its western summit being called Ngaje Ngai, which translates as House of God, such is its proximity to the heavens. During my sojourn in Tanzania with Playing for Life, we were based in Arusha and bussed every day to the parish where we were working. That bus journey was greatly enhanced if there was a break in the clouds and you could see the snow-capped peak of Kilimanjaro, a most majestic sight, rising into the sky and beckoning trekkers and mountain climbers from all around the world. I met some of them during that time in Arusha. Those who were en route to the mountain were full of anticipation, if a little nervous. Those who were returning from the climb were full of exhilaration, underlining the truth of what the German philosopher Friedrich Nietzsche had to say about mountain climbing:

"He who climbs the highest mountains laughs at all tragedies, real or imaginary."

Friedrich Nietzsche

❧

Tanzania is also blessed with other tourist attractions: Serengeti Safari Park, Lake Victoria, the island of Zanzibar. The country is one of the oldest known inhabited areas on earth, with fossil remains of human and pre-human hominids dating back two million years. It has sizeable deposits of gold and tanzanite, a light blue gemstone. Literacy levels, at 72 per cent, compare favourably with other African countries, and education is compulsory from seven to fifteen. Sounds as if Tanzania is a haven of prosperity, a jewel in the African crown. Not so for the many thousands who, to coin a phrase, are living on 'the clippings of tin'. The problem is that this is the reality for many Tanzanians. Although school leaving age is fifteen, few are still in school anywhere near that age; in fact, school attendance is put at just over half the eligible population. Many communities rely heavily on aid and, thankfully, there are groups who are willing to help out. Playing for Life, the Irish charity founded in 2006 by Tracy Piggott, has been helping out in the suburbs of Arusha, in the parish of Esso, and there are no prizes for guessing the commodity around which this little parish of two thousand people developed!

Esso is long gone from this part of Tanzania and the community is now centred around the Catholic church, and their parish priest is a Kerryman! Mike O'Sullivan hails from Milltown, outside Tralee. He trained as a chef and then decided to join the priesthood. He's middle aged, fit and energetic, devoted to his parishioners and his motorbike and they're lucky to have him. Playing for Life has been involved with the parish for a few years now and each initiative has gone from the initial stage of providing expertise and equipment to handing over the control of the initiative to the local people. That for me is a crucial element to providing aid in the developing world and the first President of Tanzania obviously felt the same way. Julius Kambarage Nyere became president following independence in 1961. In his book *Uhuru na Maendeleo* (*Freedom and Development*), which was published in 1973, he said:

"If real development is to take place,
the people have to be involved."

JULIUS KAMBARAGE NYERE

The people of Esso have certainly been involved in the development of their parish under the caring eye of Mike O'Sullivan – and with the help of the people of Ireland, who have contributed to their welfare in different ways.

A most joyous sight, at the end of my first day in the parish of Esso, was the arrival of a container which had been filled in Ireland and shipped to Tanzania six weeks previously and which was greeted with great excitement and quite a bit of manoeuvring to get it into the parish compound. At one point, it looked as if the boundary wall would have to be knocked to allow this monster to gain access to the community and I can assure you the local men would have been more than happy to oblige in order to see what was inside this vast truck. As it happened, the driver was particularly skilful and the only casualty was a mature and fruitful banana tree in the courtyard which sadly had to be chopped down to make way for this giant. Once the container was in place and the doors were opened, the excitement reached fever pitch. People came from every field and every hut to view the prizes within.

The scene was reminiscent of Christmas morning when, as a child, you'd open the sitting room door and breathe a sigh of relief that you must have been good during the year because Santa Claus had delivered the goods. I was reminded of 'Yes Virginia', the editorial published in the *New York Sun* in 1897, and which Gay Byrne read every Christmas on his radio show.

"Thank God! He lives, and he lives forever. A thousand years from now, Virginia, nay, ten times ten thousand years from now, he will continue to make glad the heart of childhood."

The contents of that container from Ireland gladdened the hearts of adults and children alike and it was all hands on deck to empty the boxes and begin the process of integrating their contents into the life of Esso parish. Twenty computers were unloaded and arranged on tables at the back of the church, ready for the IT group that would begin classes the following morning. Boxes of jam jars of all shapes and sizes were taken to Mike's kitchen to be washed, have the labels removed and sterilised in boiling water in preparation for the cookery course that would begin the following morning too. The Army School of Music had recently taken possession of new instruments and had donated the old ones to the charity so an array of musical instruments exited the container, everything from a French horn, to a tuba, a trumpet, a set of drums. The music classes were conducted by none other than Ronan Collins and

Paddy Cole, who had volunteered to travel to Tanzania to pass on their musical expertise. Sports equipment donated by the Sports Council was colourful and much admired as it appeared out of the back of the container and the children could hardly wait for their turn to use the various bits and pieces the following day in school. There were other items like bicycles, copybooks, pens and pencils which would be put to good use in the parish.

The following morning when our bus arrived in Esso, having travelled the few miles from Arusha, we were all geared up and ready for action. IT volunteers began teaching computer skills at the back of the church. Veronica Molloy from Fethard in County Tipperary gathered the piles of sterilised jam jars and oversized cooking pots and a gas ring and took herself and her helpers under the shade of some trees where local women were sitting on plastic chairs ready to learn the secrets of preserves. Veronica was definitely the right woman for the job. She is warm, energetic and vibrant, a good communicator and, as well as all that, she makes jams in her farm kitchen in Tipp for sale in the Avoca shops. I found these classes really interesting. There is an abundance of certain produce in Esso – tomatoes, bananas and onions – more than the people can consume. Rather than leave the surplus to rot, Veronica devised recipes that she demonstrated to the women. They learned how to make tomato chutney, onion marmalade and banana jam. Former President Nyere, who died in 1999, would have been very pleased.

ᘓ

"A man is developing himself when he grows, or earns, enough to provide decent conditions for himself and his family; he is not being developed if someone gives him these things."

JULIUS KAMBARAGE NYERE

ᘓ

I presume Nyere would be happy to agree that the same logic applies to a woman and certainly these women in the cookery class in Esso were developed and were delighted with the skills they had learned. They went on, at the invitation of the Irish Ambassador to Tanzania, to take a stall at a Christmas market that year in Arusha. How proud and satisfied they must have felt that day. They grew the produce, they conserved it and they turned a profit from it, providing for their families. Result!

My own involvement was with the primary schools and the colourful sports equipment I mentioned earlier. A team of six of us proceeded to the schoolyard-cum-playing pitch, which was no more than a dry and very bumpy field, to be met by masses of children, squealing with delight at the prospect of the games. They were beside themselves with excitement and who can blame them. All children love to play. For these impoverished children, there was the added dimension of actually having equipment, a luxury to which they were unaccustomed. I thought of my own children and the balls and bikes and skipping ropes and tennis rackets that they had possessed when they were growing up. Nothing too extravagant, but, nevertheless, beyond the wildest dreams of these children. Some of them were barefoot; others shared a pair of shoes. It wasn't unusual to see two friends walking together, one wearing the right shoe and the other the left, neither of them of any substance. There were children wearing school uniforms and you'd wonder why they bothered because the whole front of the jumper was totally unravelled, or the shirt was minus one of its sleeves. They were proud of the fact that they had a uniform though and didn't have to go to school like some of their friends in whatever they had been given from what people on the other side of the world had donated in the yellow clothes banks. Some of the youngsters were dressed in ill-fitting and ill-matching garments, anything from a filthy communion dress to a pair of torn shorts.

I enjoyed every minute of my time organising and playing games with the children and there's no doubt the children had a ball. There was, however, a serious side to the exercise. The games were devised to impart a message to these children about the dangers of HIV/AIDS, to teach them how the virus spreads and how stricken people are ostracised from their community, in the hope that they would avoid the disease and break the cycle of destruction, in the hope that they wouldn't end up like the people in the hospice for the dying in Monrovia, smelling of death and waiting for the release it would provide.

We also wanted to increase their self-esteem so that they would have the confidence to say no to sexual advances. One and a half million Tanzanians are living with HIV/AIDS, 15 per cent of whom are aged between fifteen and twenty-four. Some of the children we were playing with in Esso would be coming up to that age now. I hope they managed to avoid falling into that death trap. They were attentive to our words, which were translated for them by their teachers who were happy to be a part of the exercise and the fun. We left the equipment and the manuals we used with the schools so they could continue the games and the message which they shouldn't have to hear, but because of the accident of birth that saw them born into this country on this continent with this killer virus, they must be careful.

There was activity in every corner of Esso parish during the visit of Playing for Life. There were the cookery classes in the shade of the trees, the primary-school children playing games in the field while the older students took part in a drama group in a banana grove. This was a great success also and gave these teenagers an avenue for self-expression and great pride when they put on their play for their families and us on our last day there. The church was busy also with the computer skills classes. I think you could call that an example of the Church in action! And the priest's courtyard was alive with the sound of music! They were humble beginnings, but it wasn't long before Ronan and Paddy had a brass band going that rocked and could be heard I'd say back in Arusha. One thing is certain – the music served to enhance the already happy atmosphere in the parish of Esso. And the parish continues to thrive under the watchful and loving eye of this hardworking and unassuming man from the Kingdom of Kerry. I know it's a drop in the ocean. There are, after all, only two thousand people living there but it's a start and adheres to Mother Teresa's policy:

"Don't think about numbers.
Just help one person at a time."

MOTHER TERESA

I was pleased with the work that was done by Playing for Life in Tanzania and particularly with the fact that the people have taken ownership of the initiative and continue to integrate it into their community. What has happened in Esso gives the lie to a Tanzanian proverb that seems to me to point to a less than optimistic view of Western aid:

> *"I pointed out to you the stars, the moon,*
> *and all you saw was the tip of my finger."*
>
> TANZANIAN PROVERB

The parishioners of Esso and the Playing for Life volunteers have seen beyond the tip of each other's fingers. They have, together, reached for the stars and seen the beauty of the moon. Both sets of lives have been touched positively by this coming together of two cultures, both have received and both have given. Once again, Mother Teresa hit the nail on the head when she was talking about her dealings with the poor in Calcutta:

"The poor give us much more than we give them.
They're such strong people ...
We have so much to learn from them."
Mother Teresa

There was learning on both sides in Esso. The locals learned valuable new skills and the Irish volunteers learned that it is in giving that we receive. They left for home with the feeling of a job well done, a service rendered, friendships formed and life lived in a meaningful and positive way.

Africa is a continent of great diversity and contrast. There's enormous hardship and sadness but there is also great enterprise and joy. The people are poor and struggle to provide for themselves and their families, but the people are resilient, particularly the women. I visited a hut in Ethiopia at the invitation of the *bean an tí* and was lost in admiration for the way she had nothing by our terms but had an adequately equipped home by her standards. There was a mattress in the sleeping room that the whole family shared. A clothes line with a net curtain provided a screen between it and the storage area where there was an array of cardboard boxes with the essentials. Cooking and eating happened outdoors. I was really impressed by the woman's ingenuity though when I saw in different areas of the circular thatched hut, or *toukel,* different parts of a two-litre plastic bottle. It had been cut and the base was used as a cup, the body of the bottle was divided in two, each piece being placed around saplings outside to protect them from the hungry goats. The neck of the bottle fashioned a viable and very useful funnel and she used the cap to give her tiny baby sips of water. That's five uses from a discarded plastic bottle. That's enterprising in my book.

We do well to remember that where we end up on this planet is an accident of birth, and as members of the same human race with the same family instincts it's our responsibility to help where we can and provide people in the poorer parts of the world with the means to develop, so that their struggles will lessen and they will have comfort in their lives. Wouldn't it be nice if we played our part in some small way so that Nelson Mandela's dream might come true:

"I dream of an Africa which is in peace with itself."

NELSON MANDELA

God's People

"Some go to church to see and be seen,
Some go there to say they have been,
Some go there to sleep and nod,
But few go there to worship God."

I was at Mass yesterday and the homily centred around the fact that it's important, from time to time, to step back from our lives and examine them, to see where we're going, what things are important, what things need changing and, of course, given that this was the sermon at Sunday mass, what place God has in our lives. I have, at different times, fitted into all the categories described in those lines above. I like to have a look around when I go into a church. It's interesting to see the age profile and the male–female divide. I enjoy going to mass in different parts of the country and seeing the different ways people participate. For instance, yesterday in Kilkenny, the pre-Communion children were invited by the priest to go into a Sunday School-type setup to the side of the altar from which they emerged after the Liturgy of the Word. They then stood in a semi-circle on the altar, facing the congregation, to recite the Our Father before going back to their families, proudly waving the drawings of the biblical scenes they had coloured. I liked that practice. I'm sure their parents did too. It beats trying to make four- and five-year-olds sit still and be quiet in wooden pews in an oversized, echoey space.

I have often gone to Mass out of a sense of duty when I really hadn't wanted to discommode myself. This stage applied when the children were smaller and I felt, as their mother, that I should bring them and be seen to follow the rules. They were, after all, born into the Catholic Church, baptised, received Holy Communion and Confirmation and my father had a favourite saying which applies in those circumstances:

"When you enlist, you soldier."

I was, as I've already said, brought up in a traditional Catholic home. My mother, in particular, was a woman of deep faith. My father was a practising Catholic too, but he didn't collect prayers and inspirational thoughts in a copybook, so it's difficult to know how deep his faith was. I was the eldest at twenty-one and only starting to make sense of the world when he died. He was a very hard worker in the Church and in the community, a practical member of the Church if you like, who organised the parish envelope collection, visited patients in Peamount TB Hospital with his local conference of St Vincent de Paul, was a founder of Clondalkin Credit Union and Muintir na Tíre and loved to act in the Clondalkin Amateur Dramatic Society. I think my father would espouse the thinking of Bridget Willard, a modern worship leader and author in the United States who said of the Church:

"Church isn't where you meet.
Church isn't a building.
Church is what you do.
Church is who you are.
Church is the human outworking of the person of Jesus Christ. Let's not go to Church.
Let's be the Church."

BRIDGET WILLARD

My parents were married on 8 September. They chose that date because it's Our Lady's birthday. That would have been important to them, and to many young couples in Ireland at that time, if the number of people who got married on that date is anything to go by. While I was reading through my mother's copybook, I came across a letter, dated 24 October 1953, six weeks after the wedding. It was written and signed by 'Sr. M. Carina', her friend and former work colleague who had left the College of Science, become a nun and gone off teaching on the Missions in what was then called Natal, now KwaZulu-Natal province in South Africa. The letter refers to the date of the wedding:

"What a lovely day – 8th September – I feel sure that Our Lady asked many graces for you and that she could not be refused anything on her birthday."

SR CARINA

What a sweet thought. And one that would have appealed greatly to my mother. She and her friend would have been of like mind. In fact, I also learned from the letter that my mother had gone to St Patrick's Purgatory, the place of pilgrimage on Lough Derg in County Donegal, prior to her marriage:

"I well know how you prayed about it all and just imagine going to Lough Derg for the final touch! Yes God must be very pleased about it all and I feel sure that He and His Blessed Mother will look after you through all your married life."

SR CARINA

The letter isn't devoid of day-to-day chat either. There's lots of talk about my mother's talent for dressmaking and sewing and the delights of doing up a new house. There's talk of life and mores in South Africa, and a visit to Johannesburg to see her eighty-year-old aunt, also a nun. There's reminiscence about the pals at work, and her family who found it very hard to see her leave her job and enter religious life. Those were the days when people left for the Missions and didn't contemplate or dare to hope for a visit back home. I never met Sr Carina, because she never did get home, but I feel she must have been a warm and thoughtful woman, with a sense of fun and an undeniably deep faith:

"I have no means of sending you any gift as a token of remembrance. However, as it is for Our Lord's sake that we are 7,000 miles apart, so I asked Him to take my place at your wedding. Where I would be showering down confetti on you, so I asked Him to shower down His choicest blessings on you and Tom."

SR CARINA

ↆ

My mother and her friend Sr Carina were, indeed, of like mind. There's a gentle and comforting feel to the way the letter is written and the sentiments expressed. I have no doubt Mam was pleased to have those prayers and blessings on her marriage. She took her duties very seriously and we were all brought up as practising Catholics. She had a strong sense of responsibility, but she would never have felt she was discommoding herself to go to Mass. If she did, she would hardly have attended daily Mass. Her day started at seven o'clock in the morning when she came into the kitchen to put the porridge she had soaked overnight into a saucepan over a low heat before leaving the house twenty minutes later to drive to the church for 'half seven Mass'. Every day. Regular as clockwork. It set her up for the day in the same way as an early morning walk or run would appeal to people nowadays. I have to admit, in my case, I was sometimes a reluctant attendee and did have to discommode myself to get there on occasion, but I have always had the sense of responsibility when my children were in their formative years that brought us to Mass, and they accepted that with varying degrees of reluctance, depending on what they were planning for their Sunday.

I'm sure I have nodded off on occasion at Mass. I do it everywhere else, so why should the church be any different? I only have to sit into the seat in the cinema and sometimes in a theatre to feel my eyes getting heavier and eventually closing. I'm also conscientious about pulling into the hard shoulder if I feel tired while driving and given the amount of driving I do for *Nationwide*, that happens quite a lot. The funny thing is that I have no difficulty falling asleep instantly in trains, planes or automobiles, or indeed in cinemas, theatres, churches if I'm really tired, but the same rule sadly doesn't apply when I get into bed at night. I am not a good sleeper but I can cat nap at the drop of a hat. As regards nodding off in a church, I find it a most relaxing and gentle place to be. It soothes my tired spirit and if that leads to forty winks, so be it. I don't feel the need to be reciting prayers in the church building. I just want to be there and feel the comfort of having chosen to be there in the silence and the stillness:

❦

"When anyone asks me how I pray, my simple answer is that I rest in the presence of God."

SR STAN

❦

Those words of Sr Stan pretty well explain the way I feel when I go into a church, and if I close my eyes and nod off, I reckon it's a good indicator that I am indeed glad to be there and at peace. The same sentiment, more or less, is expressed by the satirical social commentator Kurt Vonnegut Jr, who'll be well known to people who've come across his works *Breakfast of Champions*, *Cat's Cradle* or *Slaughterhouse-Five*. Kurt is of the opinion that:

❦

"People don't come to church for preachments, of course, but to daydream in the presence of God."

KURT VONNEGUT JR

❦

There's nothing wrong with daydreaming either. It brings peace and joy into people's lives depending on the circumstances. I don't think God would object.

I think it's a bit harsh to say that 'few go there to worship God'. I believe that the very act of going to church is an act of worship, of observance and an endorsement of certain values in life and an aspiration to adhere to certain tenets of good living. There's not a lot wrong with that. There are many ways to worship God. I believe that my father's work in the parish was an act of worship and I believe that my mother's praying and singing in the church choir was too. They are very different pursuits, important and valuable. They are prayers in fact. To quote Sr Stan again:

"Prayer is not a question of straining the mind: it is a simple matter of opening the heart."

SR STAN

As I step back and examine my life, I can say that at this middle stage, I am happy to attend Mass most Sundays but there are occasions when I choose to visit my parents' grave instead, to visit somebody in hospital instead, to attend a different spiritual ceremony. Maybe I'm wrong, but I don't think God will mind. I remember the words of Cardinal Newman concerning correct and proper observance of religion:

"I sought to hear the voice of God
And climbed the topmost steeple.
But God declared: Go down again –
I dwell among the people."

CARDINAL NEWMAN

Sound, good sense there, no 'notions of upperosity' as Seán O'Casey might have said. These are the words of a very holy man. John Henry Newman was originally a Church of England clergyman before he converted to Catholicism and was made a cardinal in 1879. He was one of the leading figures in nineteenth-century religious life in England and was beatified by Pope Benedict XVI in September 2010 during his visit to Britain. He is also the man responsible for the hymn that has become synonymous with the final moments on board the *Titanic*. 'Lead, Kindly Light' was sung as the ill-fated ship sank on its maiden voyage in April 1912:

"Lead, kindly Light, amidst th'encircling gloom,
Lead Thou me on!
The night is dark and I am far from home,
Lead Thou me on!"

CARDINAL NEWMAN

Cardinal Newman realised that the message of Christianity necessitates being in touch with the people, living among them, helping them. He realised that there aren't too many people perched on the 'topmost steeple'. He was enlightened and wise to the fact that God dwelt among the people. This from a man of deep, unwavering faith:

"Regarding Christianity, ten thousand difficulties do not make one doubt."

CARDINAL NEWMAN

When I read about people like Cardinal Newman, who died in 1890, and realise how compassionate and wise he was, I am consoled in a way that makes me value the Church to which I belong, even though I despise and abhor the atrocities that have been committed within, some of those 'ten thousand difficulties'. It was Cardinal Newman who asserted that:

"It is almost the definition of a gentleman to say that he is one who never inflicts pain."

CARDINAL NEWMAN

I wonder what he would make of the reports like Ryan and Murphy and the awful, horrible accounts contained therein. I presume he would be as broken hearted as all right-thinking people who cannot comprehend the awfulness of what was visited on innocent children by religious entrusted with their care. I have met some of the survivors of clerical and institutional abuse and the emotions that rise up in me are of sorrow and anger. My heart goes out to the people who were robbed of their childhood happiness and who, as adults, are trying to put their lives back together. It's a very difficult process. There is no way of getting over a hell such as they endured. Herbert Ward, an Australian physician who served in the Allied Medical Corps in the First and Second World Wars, described it well when he said:

"Child abuse casts a shadow the length of a lifetime."

HERBERT WARD

It breaks my heart to think of the cruelty that was the daily routine for children in Goldenbridge Orphanage in Inchicore, a building I passed on the fifty-one bus every Friday evening as a child on my way into Irish dancing classes in the city. It breaks my heart to think of the brutality suffered by young boys in the industrial school at Artane. One of those boys spent several Christmases with a family I know in Clondalkin, who were delighted to welcome him into their home to share the joy of Christmas. Those are the two institutions that come to my mind when abuse is mentioned, because they are the institutions that I was aware of, and knowing now what was happening behind those high walls to children like me, my siblings and my friends makes me want to cry. My tears of sorrow are directed towards the children who were brutalised in so many ways. My tears of anger are directed at the adults who abused them, the Sisters of Mercy in Goldenbridge and the Christian Brothers in Artane. How can anybody be so cruel, so vicious, so cold and uncaring, so hateful? Maybe the seventeenth-century French poet Jean de la Fontaine has the answer:

"Anyone entrusted with power will abuse it
if not also illuminated with the love of
truth and virtue, no matter whether he be
a prince or one of the people."

JEAN DE LA FONTAINE

There was not a shred of virtue or truth embodied in any of the perpetrators of child abuse in those institutions. They disgraced themselves, their families and the Church to which they belonged. The message of love and justice and compassion that Jesus preached went completely over their heads. It's comforting to know that there is now a Minister for Children portfolio in government but those children, adults now, will never recapture the trust, the confidence, the joie de vivre that was so cruelly taken from them. I think of my own children and I would have fought like a tiger if anything like that had happened to them. On the other hand, I

remember myself as a child and I realise that the shock and horror of that cruelty thrives in secret. I really don't think I would have had the words to tell if something like that happened to me. I also realise that that abuse was meted out to the vulnerable children.

My mother held the clergy in very high regard. When the word went around the road that the priest was visiting houses farther up, there was a mini blitz performed on our kitchen. The tablecloth was whipped off the table and replaced with a fresh one. The best china disappeared from the china cabinet in the sitting room and magically reappeared in the kitchen cupboards. If there was time, an apple tart would be thrown together or a batch of buns put in the oven. Maybe that's where I get my fairy cake obsession from!

Mind you, Mam held the doctor in equally high regard. Many's the time I was sick in bed and yet was hauled out so that she could change the sheets before Doctor O'Higgins made his house call. When that job was done and the patient was allowed back into the admittedly very enticing freshly starched sheets, the hoover would be hauled up the stairs to give the bedroom 'a lick' and she would reverse out of the room and hoover the stairs on her way back down to the hall! My mother was of her time, and I don't doubt that that little drama was performed in many other houses around the country prior to the visit of the priest or the doctor. The women were proud of their homes and wanted them to look well. They also had a sense of right and wrong, though, and I know my mother would abhor the revelations of such wrongdoing within her beloved Church. She died before the worst of it came to light.

The question for me has centred around continuing to be a part of a Church that saw such atrocities and it's been a time of toing and froing. Following the appalling revelations that seemed to get more harrowing and more brutal by the day, I felt that by going to Mass, I was, in a way, endorsing and supporting an organisation that should be abolished. As I walked up the hill to my local church, I felt very strange. I felt unsure. What was I doing here? Did I really want to have any association with this organisation that was capable of such atrocity? I have great admiration for Andrew Madden who as a young altar boy in Dublin was abused over a three-year period by Fr Ivan Payne. When he reported this abuse, he wasn't taken seriously. Fr Payne was moved to different parishes in which he continued his evil and vicious behaviour. Andrew was the first person who suffered clerical abuse to go public. When, in 1995, he did this, he had to forfeit his anonymity in order to tackle the denials that were being offered in response to his allegations. Finally, after years of campaigning came the eventual conviction of Fr Payne and the establishment of enquiries into clerical abuse. This progress was due in no small part to Andrew's determined pursuit of justice, and, in January 2010, he decided that the right course of action for him was to leave the Catholic Church:

"I have been a Catholic in name only for many years, but after all I have seen of the Church in recent times, I decided I did not want that organisation in my life anymore, even in name only."

ANDREW MADDEN

I can understand why Andrew Madden chose to defect from the Catholic Church. He has suffered enormously and on a positive note he has continued to be a clear and energetic spokesperson for the survivors of abuse. Spirituality is still an important part of his life:

"Today, I try to hand my will and my life over to the care of that higher power every morning before I leave the house in order that my actions and thoughts might be guided by my higher power's will for me. At night I review my day and thank my higher power for everything."

Andrew Madden

❧

It's clear that Andrew Madden has shown great strength of character in the way he has regained his confidence and his dignity and he has made an important contribution to the righting of enormous wrongs. He had right on his side, he took on the system and he won. I have no doubt it was a painful and an arduous, uphill struggle. His decisive action reminds me of a piece of advice I came upon in one of Maya Angelou's books:

❧

"If you don't like something, change it.
If you can't change it, change your attitude.
Don't complain."

Maya Angelou

❧

Andrew Madden falls into the first category here. He has changed what he didn't like. He deserves every praise for having the courage of his convictions and for taking a stand against injustice that was visited upon him and so many other innocent children. It's a shame this had to happen to him, who as a young boy dreamed of becoming a priest when he grew up.

I think I fall into the second category here. I have changed my attitude. I have decided that I want to continue as a member of the Catholic Church but I am prepared to voice my objections to things that I dislike about it. There is absolutely no way I would have written a chapter like this four years ago, at the time *Lines I Love* was published. God knows, we were all aware of those same scandals then, but I think I was still vacillating, not really sure that it was possible to denounce those actions and still remain faithful to the organisation. Now I am quite happy to decry badness and raise objections to any aspects of the Church that I disagree with, while remaining within the fold. The confidence of middle age perhaps. I really don't care what people think of what I have to say as long as I feel, in my heart and soul, that what I say is right, fair and just. I think it's also due to the fact that I know many good, caring people

within the Church; some of them are priests, some of them are lay Catholics, all of them hate the badness in exactly the same way as I do, and with the same amount of heartbreak and sadness.

The other reason I'm content to remain a part of the Catholic Church is as a result of a trip to the Holy Land. The *Nationwide* Christmas programme two years ago came from Jerusalem and Bethlehem. Being in the places that I had read about and hearing the stories of Jesus made me very aware of the humanity of this man who lived in those parts two thousand years ago. He lived a life of service and of love and compassion and everywhere you go in the Holy land you sense those qualities. It's as if it's wafting in the air. It's a very holy place and I felt I was stepping into the pages of history, a history that has been the cornerstone of a civilisation. We stayed in Jerusalem, just outside the Old City overlooking the Damascus Gate. It was a busy few days, with very early starts to film enough material to fill a full *Nationwide* programme which would give our audience a sense of this place that we hear about today in terms of conflict, but which holds the essence of the Christmas message. It was a physically demanding and strenuous experience, but that paled into insignificance when compared with the emotional impact of those few days in the Holy Land. It's a crossroads to different cultures and religions. There are reminders everywhere that Christianity, Judaism and Islam share a common forefather and that the ancient city of Jerusalem began as a small settlement in the hills of Mount Moriah, mentioned in the Old Testament as the site where Isaac was nearly sacrificed by Abraham, his father and ours, whether we're Jewish, Christian or Muslim.

The Old City of Jerusalem is walled and very compact. Mark Twain visited Israel in 1867 and he was surprised by its size:

"A fast walker could go outside the walls of Jerusalem and walk entirely around the city in an hour. I do not know how else to make one understand how small it is."

MARK TWAIN

What Jerusalem lacks in size, it makes up for in history. For Jews, the connection to the city is ancient and powerful. No matter where they are in the world, Jews pray in the direction of Jerusalem. In fact, on our flight from London to Tel Aviv, at certain times some Orthodox Jewish passengers stood in the aisle to read the Torah, facing in the direction of Jerusalem. The city is constantly mentioned in prayers, and every year members of the Jewish community, no matter where they are in the world, close the Passover service with the words: 'Next year in Jerusalem.'

For those lucky enough to make it to Jerusalem, the focal point is the Western Wall, all that remains of the Second Temple, destroyed in AD 70 by the Romans. This is the holiest location of all in Judaism. It's where Jews come to mourn the destruction of their temple, hence the Wailing Wall. Every crevice is stuffed with a paper with petitions written on it. *Nationwide* got special permission to film at the Wall on Friday morning, before it is closed to all except members of the Jewish community on the eve of the Sabbath. I was struck by the fervour of the people praying there. They approach the wall, they read from the Torah, while swaying backwards and forwards and they reverse away from the wall when they're finished their prayers, rather than turn their back on this holiness. There are aspects of this practice that did not appeal to me at all. For a start, the wall is segregated, men on one side and women on the other. Also the Ultra Orthodox community struck me as extreme. They don't work, are supported by the state and their mission is to pray and procreate. They are strictly orthodox in their dress too. The men and boys have long ringlets and felt hats. The women must not reveal their hair in public so they wear hats or wigs.

And all dress from head to toe in black. Far too extreme and lacking any joie de vivre for me. At the Western Wall though, I did find myself mentally complimenting the less extreme members of the Jewish community for their observance and commitment to their faith and wondering about my own sometimes lazy approach to mine. Benjamin Disraeli described that atmosphere of observance and commitment well:

"Rome represents conquest;
Faith hovers over the towers of Jerusalem."

BENJAMIN DISRAELI

Wonder gave way to awe as we visited the Christian parts of Jerusalem. That's when my history came alive for me and with it a whole host of emotions. No matter how strong or weak your faith is, it's historical fact that a man called Jesus lived, dedicated his life to the service of others and was crucified as a result. I walked in the Garden of Gethsemane, a small park in Jerusalem, remarkable for its olive trees, some of which are three thousand years old. Its entrance is just off a side street and this is where Jesus and his disciples came following supper, the Last Supper as we now know it. He asked his friends to 'stay here and keep watch with me'. Jesus prayed, his disciples fell asleep, Judas Iscariot betrayed him to the soldiers and he was arrested. There's a feeling of sadness and stillness in the garden, despite the noise of traffic over the wall. I tried to imagine the turmoil that this man was experiencing and the confusion of his disciples, who had yet to realise what lay in store over the next twenty-four hours. Jesus said to them:

"My heart is overwhelmed with sorrow
to the point of death."

JESUS

A few hundred metres from the Garden of Gethsemane is the Tomb of Our Lady. It's underground, covered by the Chapel of the Assumption, and you walk down a series of steps, cross a courtyard and enter into this holy place which bears no resemblance to any church I had ever been in before. The reason for that is it's under the care of the Greek and Armenian Orthodox churches and their way of decorating a place of worship is very different to a Catholic's. The crypt is dark and the ceiling is blackened by rows of candles in gold, silver and red lamps, suspended on chains. There is a lot of velvet and lace around the various niches in the tomb. On the right, as you enter, there's one to honour Mary's parents, Anne and Joachim, and on the left a niche to St Joseph. Mary's tomb is in the centre, also covered by ornate materials. It's believed that it was from this spot that the Assumption took place, twenty-four hours after Mary was laid in her tomb. The smell of incense is strong, and the crypt, whose walls are solid rock, is full of chains holding hanging lamps, icons and niches.

The feeling that came over me when I visited there was of confusion about the way I grew up viewing my Catholic way of worship as the only correct way to live. When I broke a rule, I felt huge guilt. In Mary's tomb, I was very conscious of the common religious threads we share. Not only is this holy place, dedicated to Our Lady, under the care of the Greek and Armenian Orthodox churches, it is also a place of worship for Muslims. They believe that Muhammad saw a light over the tomb of 'his sister Mary' during his Night Journey to Jerusalem. Isn't it a pity that there is such emphasis on the differences between religious persuasions rather than on the fact that we have so much in common? What's important is that we live our lives as Jesus would have, loving and helping each other and enjoying the gifts and the pleasures that come our way.

Wonder, awe, sadness and confusion were joined by unbelievable heartache on Friday afternoon at three o'clock when we joined the hundreds of pilgrims who walk the Via Dolorosa at that time every week. Even though we were filming and running ahead of the crowd from time to time to be able to film the procession, I was all the time thinking how back-breakingly painful this journey must have been for a man who had been scourged and tortured, had thorns sticking into his forehead, blood flowing down his face, and was carrying a heavy wooden cross on his back. The mind boggles.

The Way of the Cross is organised and led by the Franciscan community in Jerusalem. They lead the procession in prayer and stop at each of the Stations of the Cross, which are marked by plaques on the wall. It's a steep-enough climb through narrow streets with traders on either side. I wondered why it hadn't been cleared of little shops and then realised that Jesus had to make his way through crowds of people on that Friday afternoon. The trade and hustle and bustle of daily life on the Via Dolorosa continues uninterrupted today, just as it did two thousand years ago.

"A large number of people followed him,
Including women who mourned and wailed for him."

LUKE 23:27

ᘓ

The heartache that I felt at the thought of any man having to struggle in pain along narrow winding roads reached its zenith when we reached the top of the hill and entered the Church of the Holy Sepulchre. I crossed the yard, went through the doors and every image I had ever held of Calvary from the time I was a child came flooding back to me. And it's not because Golgotha bears any resemblance to the images we see of Calvary. Quite the opposite. It's a large cavernous church. Steps to the right bring you up to what was the top of the hill, the place where Jesus was crucified, alongside two other men. This is marked by an altar with a huge crucifix reaching up into the heavens. It's lavishly decorated with gold and silver which is not surprising in that it's under the control of the Greek Orthodox community. In fact, the Church of the Holy Sepulchre is the headquarters of the Patriach of Greek Orthodoxy, its control and maintenance is shared by several Christian churches and is home to Eastern Orthodoxy, Oriental Orthodoxy and Roman Catholicism.

The story is the same, though, no matter through whose eyes it is viewed. On that spot three crosses stood, and Jesus was nailed to the middle one. On either side, two men convicted of robbery:

❦

"We are punished justly, for we are getting what our deeds deserve. But this man has done nothing wrong."

❦

And the words of that robber were ringing in my ears as I descended the steps from Golgotha back into the body of the church to view The Stone of Unction, on which Joseph of Arimathea is supposed to have prepared Jesus for burial in the tomb which is inside The Rotunda over to the left:

❦

"Jesus, remember me when You come into Your kingdom."

❦

That visit to Jerusalem helped me to change my attitude to my Church. It's a diverse, ancient place where the message of Christianity was brought home to me in a way that opened my mind to the fact that it's not the exclusive domain of Roman Catholics. I realise we've always known this in theory, but there has been a tendency within our Church to feel a bit superior. My visit to Jerusalem showed me that any feeling of superiority would be totally alien to Jesus – the loving and caring person who walked that land two thousand years ago – that feeling of superiority and misplaced entitlement which is outlined in the pages of the Murphy and Ryan reports.

That's not to say that Jerusalem, Israel and The Holy Land are without their own problems. In the words of David K. Shipler, the American writer who won the Pulitzer Prize in 1987 for his book, *Arab and Jew: Wounded Spirits in a Promised Land*:

"Jerusalem is a festival and a lamentation.
Its song is a sigh across the ages, a delicate,
robust, mournful psalm at the great junction
of spiritual cultures."

DAVID K. SHIPLER

ᘛ

The conflict between Palestinians and Jews bubbles beneath the surface in Jerusalem. Relations are strained in East Jerusalem, with Jews being housed in areas which had been designated as Arab neighbourhoods. To travel to and from Bethlehem, you must pass through an army checkpoint leaving Jerusalem. We were waved through every time. On one occasion, there was a long queue and it transpired there was a row at the checkpoint with Palestinians being searched and delayed, unnecessarily in their opinion, as they hurried to work in Jerusalem. Echoes of a border closer to home perhaps?

A twenty-foot-high concrete wall covered in graffiti is one of the first things that greets you as you leave the checkpoint and the city of Jerusalem behind you. It's to prevent attack by suicide bombers. It's ugly and not dissimilar to other concrete walls in Germany and here in our own country. Not a very pleasing introduction to Bethlehem, which is a pity given the significance of the place. You'd have to have a heart of stone to be unmoved by the experience of standing in Manger Square, looking towards the Church of the Nativity, contemplating the birth of Jesus underneath its roof. Underneath its

floor also as it happens, because Mary and Joseph were given shelter with the animals and they were housed traditionally underground in those days. To view the manger you bend down low and descend steps which open out into a cave under the altar. A silver star marks the spot where the baby lay and every year, millions of pilgrims from all Christian faiths and from all parts of the globe lay their palm on that silver star and offer a silent prayer:

"Away in a manger, no crib for His bed,
the little Lord Jesus laid down His sweet head.
The stars in the bright sky looked down where He lay,
the little Lord Jesus asleep in the hay."

JAMES R. MURRAY

That lovely warm feeling of joy that we experience at Christmas is everywhere in Bethlehem – in the square, in the church and in the souks manned by happy, friendly people selling their wares. Lucinda Franks, the former *New York Times* reporter and the first woman to win the Pulitzer Prize for reportage, described her experience of Bethlehem:

ꝏ

"The ancient dream: a cold clear night made brilliant by a glorious star, the smell of incense, shepherds and wise men falling to their knees in adoration of the sweet baby, the incarnation of perfect love."

LUCINDA FRANKS

ꝏ

That's the way I view my attachment to the Catholic Church now. I have changed my attitude and I refuse to be dragged down by the awfulness of what was perpetrated by horrible people. I try to live my life in accordance with what Jesus, 'the incarnation of perfect love', would have wanted.

There are so many good people working in the Church today. It's a shame for them that others acted in unjust and disgusting ways and brought shame on their calling. There are many who will say I'm an à la carte Catholic. They're right. And do you know what? That's the way I like it. There are too many Church rules that are at odds with what Jesus would have wanted. There's a guest house in East Jerusalem, set up by the Catholic Church following a meeting between Pope Paul VI and Monsignor Jean Rodhain, the founder of the French charity Secours Catholique (Caritas France). The pope asked the monsignor to establish a house in Jerusalem for the poor. The site was provided by the patriach of the Syrian Catholics. It had been a Benedictine Priory, a Syrian seminary and was now to become a hotel. It was taken over by Secours Catholique in 1964 and set about accomplishing its mission – welcoming pilgrims from all religious backgrounds and helping the poor of Jerusalem. The director is an Irishman, a priest from County Clare. As well as the guest house, they provide free medical care and medicine for the poor of East Jerusalem. It's called Abraham's House, and as Monsignor Rodhain defined it back in 1964:

"As its name suggests, Abraham's House has a special goal: it is a house that is open to all Abraham's children."

Monsignor Rodhain

And that, for me, is the way of the future.

Pilgrim's Progress

"For in their hearts doth Nature stir them so
Then people long on pilgrimage to go
And palmers to be seeking foreign strands
To distant shrines renowned in sundry lands."

GEOFFREY CHAUCER

Little did I think as I sat listening to John Fanagan, one of my English lecturers when I was in First Year Arts in UCD, extolling the virtues of *The Canterbury Tales*, that I would one day return to Chaucer's masterpiece because I had developed an interest in pilgrimage and undertaken one or two myself. I have to be honest and say that, at the time, John Fanagan's lecture was not the highlight of my week. I would rather have stuck pins in my eyes than sit listening to more extracts from the different tales on the road to Canterbury. It was written at the end of the fourteenth century in Middle English, with weird spellings, and is the tale of thirty people taking the pilgrim route from Southwark to the shrine of St Thomas a'Becket in Canterbury, a motley crew indeed. Among them a knight, a miller, a man of law, a physician, a merchant, a squire, a wife of Bath, the nun's priest and many more. Each had their own tale, and it was hard work at eighteen years of age to summon up an interest in their lives and their stories:

"They brought a cook for this occasion, who
With marrow-bones would boil their chicken stew,
With powder-marchant tart and galingale.
Well could he judge a draught of London ale.
And he could roast and seethe and broil and frye,
And brew good soup, and well could make a pie."

GEOFFREY CHAUCER

I know you're probably chomping at the bit to find out more about the cook and his accomplishments and capabilities, but you'll have to read the *Tales* yourself to find out what happened next. I've had enough already. After all, I was from Clondalkin on the outskirts of Dublin, feeling a bit out of my depth in university in the first place and, secondly, diversity of interests was not my strong suit at that stage. I didn't need to read about cooks and pardoners and their pals and their exploits in indecipherable English. To be fair to Mr Fanagan, he was young, enthusiastic and he certainly brought the stories to life by highlighting the salient points in the vernacular of the twentieth century. He was a very funny and lively teacher and I suppose the irony of those qualities, given the fact that he was part of the Fanagan family of undertakers, was not lost on me. I did, reluctantly, attend all his lectures. I was too scared not to. I was a nerd after all and devoured every piece of information at lectures and in the library, just to be sure to be sure that I would pass the first-year exams. My confidence did increase as the years went on, but I don't think I ever relaxed enough to enjoy college life. In fact, I'd love to go back and study there at this stage in life and relish the work and also the ambience. Maybe I'll put that on my bucket list!

Back to Chaucer and his *Canterbury Tales*. I have travelled to a few 'distant shrines in foreign lands' and each time I do, I remind myself of sitting in that lecture theatre in Belfield, not understanding the value of the piece of writing or the journey depicted therein. All that has changed, thankfully, because there is something very wholesome and very satisfying about pilgrimage, physically, spiritually and emotionally, and the knowledge that people have been doing it for centuries, and in all sorts of different circumstances, is very humbling. Humility is one of the cornerstones of pilgrimage too. It's difficult to have notions of grandeur when you're walking around in cold weather in your bare feet, as is the requirement on Lough Derg, St Patrick's Purgatory. Patrick Kavanagh describes it well:

"Lough Derg, St Patrick's Purgatory in Donegal,
Christendom's purge."

PATRICK KAVANAGH

I've been there twice. The first visit, at the tender age of seventeen, was to pray for good Leaving Cert results. Mind you, the pilgrimage happened after the exams so in practical terms, the die had been cast. I was banking on the fact that I had made the promise to go there prior to sitting the papers. It was a memorable experience. I can remember every detail as if it were yesterday. The rain, the damp clothes in the dormitory and the condensation on the window, the dry toast that stuck to my palate, the bitter black tea, the awful tiredness, my feet being so cold that my mother wrapped newspapers around them during the all-night vigil and the praying. The highlight of the three-day pilgrimage was the journey home when the bus stopped north of the border and we bought Opal Fruits, a rare treat, unavailable in the Republic at the time. Indulge me here folks, I was only seventeen. It was all I could do to hold them intact, unopened, until midnight when the fast officially ended. Then it was party time, Opal Fruits time! It was a tough three days and I didn't offer to accompany my mother on any more of her frequent visits to the island.

I never forgot it though, and I was delighted when it was suggested that we film a *Nationwide* special from Lough Derg in 2010. It was an opportunity to compare the two visits. They couldn't have been more different and not just because of the thirty plus years of a gap between the two trips. First of all, it didn't rain. The sun even shone for a little while, although it was pretty cold at night-time and I felt sorry for the pilgrims on their all-night vigil. I wasn't doing the pilgrimage this time around. It's not really possible to combine both disciplines I think. That's my story anyway and I'm sticking to it! Being relieved of footwear on arrival at the pier made sense to me this time around, whereas when I was seventeen, I thought it was just another gratuitous act of torture to make us suffer more. Everyone is equal on the pilgrimage. Prince or pauper, man or woman, young or old, it makes no difference. Everyone is barefoot, everyone follows the same routine of prayer, everyone is fasting. It's physically demanding, a tough three days of pilgrimage. Patrick Kavanagh doesn't put a tooth in it in his poem 'Lough Derg':

❦

"Women and men in bare feet turn again
To the iron crosses and the rutted Beds,
Their feet are swollen and their bellies empty."

PATRICK KAVANAGH

❦

Everyone sleeps in dormitories and is very glad of it, by the way, after the night vigil, spent walking in circles around St Patrick's Basilica, praying the Rosary, with breaks which are spent in the night shelter with a cup of soup. 'Soup!' you say. Sure that's no hardship then. I'm talking about Lough Derg soup and you won't be finding the recipe for it in any Neven Maguire or Rachel Allen cookbook. Nor would you be interested in looking for the recipe. Lough Derg soup consists of hot water with salt and pepper. Nothing to write home about for sure, but it's hot and has a bit of a kick in it thanks to the addition of the condiments. I can assure you it's very welcome at three or four in the morning when you're trying to get warm and stay awake. The all-night vigil made no sense to my seventeen-year-old self who saw it as yet another way to make the pilgrims suffer. Now I can see the value of ritual and walking and praying in this mantra-like way.

This continuous journey is replicated during the day with the prayerful processions around the basilica and the prayers around the different penitential beds and circular stone walls, which have been constructed from the remains of monks' cells or oratories. They're made up of boulders and rough stones, some of them are on a steep incline and in the centre of them all is a crucifix. Yeats made reference to the ritual of praying the beds in his poem 'The Pilgrim':

"Round Lough Derg's holy island
I went upon the stones,
I prayed at all the Stations upon
my matrow-bones."

W.B. YEATS

There's a rhythm to praying in this way which is comforting, I think. In fact, I have my own routine now of praying the Rosary when I go on my power walk in the mornings. This resulted from a pilgrimage I took to Medjugorje a few years ago. More of that anon. Reciting the Rosary takes care of the first ten minutes of my walk and then I daydream or plan my day for the rest of the time. I offer it for different reasons at different times. It's part of my routine, my ritual of walking, and it fits nicely into the rhythm of the walk. Did I ever think I'd see the day, when I was saying the Rosary through the bars of the kitchen chairs growing up in Clondalkin, that I would willingly recite it as I pound the pavements? More importantly, did my mother ever think such a thing would happen? I doubt it. I hope she'd be pleased. As soon as I start the walk, I decide what I want to offer the Rosary for that day and off I go. As I get older, I realise that I'm a traditionalist at heart. I'm not sure yet what good this does me but I know it does me no harm.

The people I met on Lough Derg were all offering their pilgrimage for a reason. And there were as many reasons as there were pilgrims. Two sisters decided to go because their brother was seriously ill. A young barrister in his thirties was there because his wife was expecting their first child. Two young men who had recently returned to Ireland from working abroad were there to pray for a job. A young Traveller girl was there because she was finding it difficult to conceive a child. An elderly widower was there because he had been mugged and beaten up. He told me he had forgiven his attackers but he felt the need of prayer to give him back his confidence. All had their dreams and were willing to endure a bit of hardship in the hope that these dreams would be realised. Paulo

Coelho explains the draw of the pilgrimage in his book of the same name:

❧

"It is the pleasure of searching and the pleasure of the adventure. You are nourishing something that's very important – your dreams."

PAULO COELHO

❧

I imagine all of the people that I met on Lough Derg last year would relate to the notion of searching, of adventure, of nourishing dreams. Pleasure, however, is probably not a word they or I would associate with three days on the island! There is, though, a great sense of accomplishment and satisfaction. There's no doubt that the physical aspect of pilgrimage is hugely central to the overall experience.

I've visited Fatima and Medjugorje, two well-known Marian sites, both very popular with Irish pilgrim groups, who travel there in their planeloads every year to spend time at these holy places and to pray undisturbed by the hustle and bustle of busy lifestyles. Fatima is about an hour's drive from Lisbon. Our Lady is reputed to have appeared in 1917 to three young shepherd children, ten-year-old Lucia Santos and her younger cousins, Jacinta and Francisco Marto. The first apparition was on 13 May and they followed on that same date for six consecutive months. Lucia described the woman she saw while she and her cousins were tending the sheep just outside their home village of Fatima. She was:

ᘓ

"... brighter than the sun, shedding rays of light clearer and stronger than a crystal ball filled with the most sparkling water and pierced by the burning rays of the sun."

ᘓ

You can imagine the reaction when the word got out and the children reported further apparitions on the thirteenth of the following months. By the time October came around, there was a crowd of seventy thousand people gathered to witness what the children could see. There were many reports of the sun spinning in the sky – 'The Miracle of the Sun'. A reporter who went there to cover the story for the Lisbon daily *O Dia* referred in his article to:

ᘓ

"The silver sun, enveloped in the same gauzy purple light was seen to whirl and turn in the circle of broken clouds. The light turned a beautiful blue, as if it had come through the stained-glass windows of a cathedral, and spread itself over the people who knelt with outstretched hands. People wept and prayed with uncovered heads, in the presence of a miracle they had awaited."

ꝺ

The phenomenon of Fatima was established. It has grown now to be one of the major places of pilgrimage to Our Lady. Jacinta and Francisco died a couple of years after the apparitions, in 1919 and 1920, both of them having fallen victim to the Spanish flu epidemic that hit the area. Lucia became a nun and died in 2005, at the age of ninety-seven.

One of the traditions associated with pilgrimage to Fatima is called the Holy Mile and it involves walking on your knees in the massive churchyard from the new basilica to the shrine at the apparition. I witnessed some young Spanish girls praying the Rosary as they shuffled on their knees along the Holy Mile; some of them wore kneepads and some didn't, similar, I suppose to people climbing Croagh Patrick, some barefoot, some not. Either way, it's a tough and painful exercise that people are willing to undertake as part of their pilgrimage. I know there are many who will scoff at such self-inflicted hardship with references to 'Catholic guilt' and other clichés but, at this stage in life, I live by a philosophy of 'each to his own'. If it gives comfort and sustenance to a person, what's the harm in that? I'm also constantly reminding myself and my children of Friedrich Nietzsche's philosophy:

"What doesn't kill you makes you stronger."

FRIEDRICH NIETZSCHE

A delightful aspect of the pilgrimage to Fatima for me was the candlelight procession in the evening. It was visually spectacular, with thousands of people weaving in procession into and around the churchyard and ending up at the Apparition shrine. Looking down on it from a height, it was almost carnival like, so beautiful, a mixture of candles, torches, banners and singing. Very gentle and extremely uplifting. Following the procession, I decided to light a candle. I love lighting candles, no matter what the circumstances, and if I can have my dinner table and hallway looking like the entrance to a candle factory, why not light a candle in such a holy place? For me, candles are welcoming, warming and a very nice way of remembering loved ones when visiting a church anywhere in the world. I got quite a shock when I went to light a candle in Fatima though. Forget the words 'gentle' and 'uplifting' with regard to this candle grotto. Discard any mental picture you have of long brass rows into which you place your lighted candle or little tealight. This place is a furnace. And that's the intention. One of the Three Secrets of Fatima, which Our Lady is reputed to have passed on to the young children, included a vision of Hell which was graphic and frightening:

"Our Lady showed us a great sea of fire which seemed to be under the earth. Plunged in this fire were demons and souls in human form, like transparent burning embers, all blackened or burnished bronze, floating about in the conflagration, now raised into the air by the flames, that issued from within themselves together with great clouds of smoke, now falling back on every side, like sparks in a huge fire, without weight or equilibrium, and amid

shrieks and groans of pain and despair, which horrified us and made us tremble with fear."

ᘓ

I'll bet it made them tremble with fear. I'd be horrified by such a sight. This vision of Hell is recalled in the candle grotto in Fatima. The candles you light are tall and thick and you position them in what looks like a huge skillet barbecue. The heat is oppressive. Once you've placed your candle, you must move away quickly. The flaming candles are all misshapen by the heat and running into each other. Not a pretty sight. To be avoided at all costs, and I'm not talking about the actual grotto here, if you know what I mean! Personally, I greatly disliked this aspect of Fatima. I think it's a lost opportunity to allow people to reflect in the gentle and reassuring surroundings of a collection of candles, each of them representing a prayer on behalf of somebody who needs a bit of help or support.

Medjugorje, on the other hand, has a beautiful candle grotto. It's actually a separate and sunken garden off the main churchyard, a prayerful place of peace and tranquillity, a horseshoe shape, where people come to light their candles and then sit on the benches and reflect, contemplate or just simply watch other people doing the same thing. It's a million miles from the candle grotto in Fatima. I know which one I'd choose! I've been to Medjugorje twice. The first time was by invitation to join a pilgrimage from Dublin, organised by a dear friend. I'm always interested to see new places and I was fascinated by this story of Marian apparitions, which began in 1981 and which are supposedly still daily occurrences in the lives of the visionaries who would be present during the week. I must also admit that the idea of spending a few days in sunny Bosnia-Herzegovina at the end of June was a major part of the appeal. That was a mistake! To say that it rained for most of the time doesn't really do justice to the deluge that was Medjugorje that last week in June 2009! The first thing I bought was a plastic green poncho which served me well and saw service the following month when my niece borrowed it to wear to a very wet Oxegen festival in Kildare. It was when she took it out of its bag that she discovered it had Medjugorje emblazoned big and bold along the back. She wore it though. Any port in a storm. Probably the first time that logo was displayed at Punchestown Racecourse.

The rain was ferocious in Medjugorje. I got fed up hearing how fabulous the weather is normally, that this was the first time anyone had ever seen rain. I should have warned them that everywhere I go it rains. I spent three days in Nice in July a few years ago. It rained for two of them. On one of my trips to Ethiopia, it rained

every afternoon. I travelled to Calcutta with GOAL and it lashed out of the heavens every day, and my goodness in Calcutta the rain made the already disgusting living conditions of people in the slums into a sludgy, slimy mudbath with rats and litter scuttling about. Anyway, the moral of this little rant is to be very careful not to book holidays in the sun anytime around the period I might be travelling there!

Despite the rain, Medjugorje is a very interesting place. It's small, home to about four thousand very friendly and welcoming people, although that number is swollen all year round by the pilgrims of all faiths and none who visit the town. More than one million pilgrims come every year, forty-five million in total since the beginning of the apparitions. Medjugorje is twenty-five miles from Mostar, a name we all became familiar with for the atrocities committed there during the Bosnian war in the nineties, and the fascinating aspect of this Marian location is that the visionaries are still alive. Vicka lives in Medjugorje and two of the others, Marija and Ivan, come back to their home place every year. Marija gave a talk in a packed community hall which I attended and it was interesting to hear her account of what happened on that June day thirty years ago. Two teenagers were walking just outside the town when they saw the Gospa, as Mary is referred to there. The following day, they were joined by four of their friends and they also saw her. Since that day, Our Lady has appeared daily, and once a month she gives a message that she would like imparted to the world. These messages revolve around peace, love, faith, prayer and fasting. They always begin with the words 'Dear children', and they always finish with the sentence, 'Thank you for responding to my call.'

I was introduced to Marija and she invited a few of us to be present at her apparition that evening. We went along to her house in the town, where she spends the summers with her family. She's married to an Italian businessman and has four sons. The house is comfortable, traditional, and has a nice garden with a chapel. Marija is a lovely looking woman in her forties who has the most welcoming smile imaginable. Her sister, who saw Our Lady on the first Apparition and never again, was also in the house and some of Marija's boys and their friends came in and out, looking for biscuits and other goodies. We all sat around, drinking coffee and eating cake. The conversation revolved around the apparitions, but what struck me about Marija was how she fitted this part of her life into a very busy schedule of mothering and looking after her family. Her apparition takes place at six forty every evening no matter where she is, so at about six thirty we all made our way from her kitchen-cum-

sitting-room over to her chapel. It was packed. Local people and other invited pilgrims were there, to pray with Marija and to be present for her apparition. Marija came in, knelt in front of the statue of Our Lady at the side of the altar and began giving out the Rosary. We all responded and then she just stopped speaking, joined her hands in front of her and looked heavenwards. There was no drama, all was quiet, everyone was respectful and Marija remained in what seemed like a trance for at least ten minutes. Then she came back to us and picked up the Rosary where she left off.

For every person who believes Our Lady appeared to Marija in that chapel in Bosnia that evening, there is at least one other who believes she's deluded at best and perpetuating a money-making scam at worst. I've thought about this long and hard. Having met Marija and seen her in her family setup, I believe that no busy mother and wife would bring this willingly on herself. It's disruptive to have to incorporate this into your daily life, no matter where you are in the world. Privacy is compromised, at least some of the time. I think it would be very difficult to perpetuate such a scam for thirty whole years, through teenage years, dating years, marriage and children. Marija is a genuine, lovely woman. I believe this is true for her. It brings millions of people to prayer in all parts of the world. Surely that's a good thing.

Everything revolves around prayer in Medjugorje. It's a holy place. Despite the Catholic Church failing so far to approve what happened in the town, Pope John Paul II, for instance, was always a great supporter of Medjurgorje:

"Medjugorje, Medjugorje.
It's the spiritual heart of the world."
POPE JOHN PAUL II

We stayed in a guest house run by a young local woman, Marina, and her husband, and before every meal, after the food had been laid on the table, they would stand in between the tables and lead us in saying grace. If a group of people found themselves together in the evening after dinner, somebody would suggest saying the Rosary. It seemed easy and informal. In fact, it was after that trip to Medjugorje that I decided to say the Rosary on my exercise walk. I like the feel of it as I exercise and pray at the same time, and, of course, there's lots of time left for the essential daydreaming and happy-hormone-induced positive planning! There is lots of opportunity for praying in Medjugorje. Apparition Hill is laid out with brass plates depicting the fifteen mysteries of the Rosary. It's a climb worthy of the physical aspect of pilgrimage and then there's Church Mountain, an altogether more challenging climb, with the Stations of the Cross to keep the pilgrims focused on the way up the mountain. Almost at the top of the mountain, there's a memorial to Father Slavko Barbaric, a Franciscan priest who disobeyed church orders and displayed huge devotion to the story of the apparitions. You see, Medjugorje has not been approved by the Catholic Church, although last year the Church did set up an investigative commission into the story. Too late for Father Slavko though. He climbed Church Mountain every single day, carrying a bag to pick up any litter dropped by pilgrims along the way. On 24 November 2000, just as he got to the last station, he turned to the people who had climbed with him and said:

"We will now pray for all the pilgrims in Medjugorje and we will now pray for the next one to die."

FATHER SLAVKO

He then sat down to rest and died. He was fifty-four years of age, loved and well known to all the pilgrims and the locals and there is a plaque in his memory at the spot where he died.

Many pilgrims climb both Apparition Hill and Church Mountain several times during their stay in Medjugorje. Church Mountain is a particularly strenuous climb but everyone who ascends seems to come back down with a smile on their face. As Edmund Hillary said about mountain climbing:

"It's not the mountain we conquer, but ourselves."
EDMUND HILLARY

A good reason for going on a pilgrimage that, and a nice result when we conquer not the mountain but our fears and anxieties.

There are also ceremonies in the basilica and evening celebrations and a wonderful pre-dawn procession which begins in the next town and makes its way into Medjugorje in the early morning. It's not all praying though. There are nice coffee shops in the town, and I had a wonderful massage while I was there. There's fun to be had chatting to other pilgrims. Medjugorje is hugely popular with Irish people, as is Fatima. I liked it for its simplicity. The town consists of the main street with a few other streets off it and then you're out in the country. In fact, to get to Apparition Hill you have to leave the road and walk through fields on the outskirts of the town, following the path those teenagers took when they went walking on 24 June 1981. You pass some of the cottages where the children lived and go up some winding roads to get to the base of the hill. No special arrangements, no car parks, just normal living in this rural community. Walking through those fields I was reminded of the words of Paulo Coelho in his book *The Pilgrimage*:

"It is the road that teaches us the best way to get there. And the road enriches us as we walk its length."

PAULO COELHO

I can't think of any better way to get to the hill on which these children claim to have seen Our Lady than by walking through the fields that they walked and realising that a mere thirty years ago, this phenomenon happened in the heart of a simple rural community in Bosnia-Herzegovina. The thirtieth anniversary was marked this June and *Nationwide* was there to cover the ceremonies.

The lines I quoted above from Paulo Coelho's book describe well the richness of travelling the road in Medjugorje and on other pilgrimages. He was, however, referring specifically to the road he travelled himself in the footsteps of St James, the Camino de Santiago de Compostela. This is another pilgrimage that's very popular with Irish people, although to walk a stretch of the Camino offers opportunity to meet with people from all corners of the globe such is its renown, a renown that has endured since at least the twelfth century when it rivalled Rome and Jerusalem as goals of Christian pilgrimage. Its international dimension saw a bit of a downturn between 1789 and 1815, the time of the French Revolution and the Napoleonic Wars. European pilgrims began to flock to do the Camino again after 1879 when the skull of St James, which had been hidden from the French army, was rediscovered. The story goes that St James the Apostle had spent some time after the Crucifixion preaching in Hispania, was martyred by Herod Agrippa around AD 44 and that some of his Spanish disciples brought his remains back to Spain where he was buried in what is now called Santiago.

Originally a little oratory was built over his tomb, which expanded to become a Benedictine Monastery and evolved over the years to the magnificent cathedral of Santiago, the destination for all pilgrims on the Camino de Santiago de Compostela. Archaeological excavations in 1945 revealed several tombs, among them that of St James, clearly identified by its inscription, and when it was opened it revealed a silver casket decorated with scallop shells. That shell has become the symbol of the Camino. Many pilgrims wear it around their neck, some tie it onto their rucksacks, and the concrete direction stones are marked with it.

On a recent visit to Dingle, I noticed that the low wall across the road from the Church of St James has been decorated with a series of scallop patterns and the archives of the town show that pilgrims left from there to walk the Camino de Santiago de Compostela. This discovery added a whole new dimension to my relationship with this part of Kerry, one of my favourite places in Ireland, where I fell in love with the Irish language and everything it stands for. When I became an Irish teacher, I enthused about the Dingle Peninsula at every opportunity. I am one of the few people who actually enjoyed *Peig*! I liked reading it and I liked teaching it. That enthusiasm

must have been visible to my pupils because I found out years after I finished teaching that my nickname was Peig. The same Peig was awestruck when, as a young girl, she left her home in Dun Chaoin to come into Dingle to work in Curran's shop in the town:

"Ach fé dheireadh do shroicheamar an Daingin. Ach, mo mhíle mairg, sin é an áit gur tháinig an t-ionadh ormsa. Tithe móra arda ar gach taobh díom, daoine ag imeacht tharana chéile sall is anall agus gan aon tuiscint agamsa ar a gcaint. Bhí an dá shúil ag dul as mo cheann le scranadh."

("Finally we reached Dingle. My goodness that was a big surprise. Big, tall houses on every side, people going hither and yon and I didn't understand a word of what they were saying. My two eyes were popping out of my head with fear.")

Peig Sayers

I imagine young Peig would have been even more surprised and in awe of Dingle town if she'd known it had been a starting point for one of the most important pilgrim routes in the world centuries before her arrival. A few years ago, that tradition was revived when the *Jeanie Johnston* sailed with pilgrims from Dingle to La Coruña in Spain, where they disembarked and began the long walk to Santiago.

It's certainly a long walk, somewhere in the region of eight hundred kilometres, and there are staunch souls who journey the whole way in one attempt. Most people, though, do it in stages. I walked the final hundred and fifty kilometres three years ago with a group of people, some of whom I already knew, some I was meeting for the first time – all of whom have become firm friends and we have embarked on other walking expeditions since. It was my first time to do anything like that and it was a wonderful experience. Despite the weather! I lived up to my reputation for bringing rain wherever I go. We were a group of differing levels of fitness but we were a group, so nobody was left behind. We'd start out together in the morning, agree a coffee stop and wait there until the slower walkers caught up with the rest. We didn't jump up then, eager to get going again. How mean would that be! No, civilised and well-brought-up folk that we are, we waited until they too had coffee and then we all set off together again. There were times when the going was tough but we were well ready for it, equipped with walking poles, boots and, of course, rain gear. I suppose you could say we were shining examples of the truth of a very wise old Nigerian saying:

"The day on which one starts out is not the time to start one's preparations."

NIGERIAN PROVERB

We did, however, come across some pilgrims en route who had not noted this wisdom and boy were they suffering. I walked some of the journey one day with an American girl who had taken three months out to walk the entire Camino and she was in an awful state of fatigue and blistered feet. She could hardly walk, yet she soldiered on, having arranged to meet up with friends in Santiago to go on holiday. They had flown over from the States. Clever bunnies! She's the one who walked the walk though and has the lovely ornate Latin scroll to prove it.

For me, the value of the Camino lay in the opportunity to walk a distance on a holy trail. The Camino traverses towns, villages, main roads, forests, farmland. Sometimes you can see right into people's gardens, so close is the trail to their gate. The Camino took me on an outer journey through the countryside of Galicia in northern Spain, looking in on the ordinary day-to-day lives of its people. It also took me on an inner journey of reflection on the important things in my life. This happened sometimes in silence as I walked a part of the way alone, sometimes in conversation with other members of our group. You get to know people quite well when you share a road with them.

"Giorraíonn beirt bóthar."

("Two people together shorten the journey.")

IRISH PROVERB

Friendships deepened certainly, there were exchanges of advice, reminiscences of times past, banter, the normal chitchat of everyday life. The highlight of our journey was arriving into Santiago for the Mass of Pilgrims, in glorious sunshine as it happened. That's another curiosity of my foreign travel. The clouds usually clear and the sun shines just as I'm about to return home. We passed the hideous monument to commemorate the visits of Pope John Paul II to the city in 1982 and 1989. When we looked down from the top of the hill we could see the majestic spires of the cathedral. I wondered about the millions of people over the centuries who have stood at that same point and gazed at the beauty of the city and its cathedral – footsore, hungry and weak from the long journey but exalted by the sense of awe and the sense of satisfaction at having accomplished a great feat. The Mass of the Pilgrims provided another opportunity to marvel at the diverse groups of people, of different races, of different ages, of different beliefs and with different reasons for undertaking this pilgrimage. It was a multinational celebration of endurance, piety and humanity and I felt privileged to be a part of it.

For me, a pilgrimage is an opportunity to remember and honour a special story about special people, be it the children of Fatima or Medjugorje, St James the Apostle in Santiago, Jesus Christ on the Via Dolorosa in Jerusalem or any of the other situations commemorated in other holy places here in Ireland and in other parts of the world. For every supernatural and divine occurrence in each of those stories there is also a human element, of children in simple rural villages, of a man forced to carry a cross to which He would be nailed, of another man, His friend, travelling across the seas to spread the word of His teachings. How could those human stories leave a person unmoved? They are stories of courage, of ridicule, of struggle and for the many people who honour them in pilgrimage, they are stories of hope and optimism. Pilgrimage demands effort, sometimes physical effort, but it affords a person a priceless opportunity to step outside of the daily routine and re-evaluate the important things in life, the things to cherish and hold dear. Those things are never materialistic. I came upon a tin plaque outside a tiny shop in a tiny village in Uganda while I was there with GOAL four years ago. It impressed me so much that I took a photo of it and keep it on my fridge door:

"Money can buy bed, but not sleep,
Books but not brains,
Cosmetics but not beauty,
A house but not a home,
Food but not appetite,
Religion but not salvation,
Luxuries but not culture,
A passport to anywhere,
But not to heaven."

There's a lot of sound advice contained in those words. Whoever wrote them had a good sense of what's important in life. Full marks to the shopkeeper too for attaching the plaque to his door. His sense of community obviously outweighed any desire to inveigle every last penny out of his customers. We do well to remember the veracity of that statement, and pilgrimage certainly gives you an outlook on life that puts the material in its rightful subordinate place. Charles Kingsley, the nineteenth-century English writer and clergyman, offers a similar reminder:

"We act as if comfort and luxury were the chief requirements of life, when all we need to make us really happy is something to be enthusiastic about."

CHARLES KINGSLEY

To my mind, pilgrimage is something to be enthusiastic about. It's an uplifting and educational journey and the person you learn most about on an expedition to a holy place is yourself. I'd highly recommend the experience. We're lucky in this country that we have opportunities to embark on such an expedition. Apart from Lough Derg, there's Croagh Patrick and Knock in County Mayo, the monastic sites on the Aran Islands, Skellig Michael, which fascinates me hugely. It's an inhospitable place to look at, certainly, no more than a pointed rock really, seven hundred feet about sea level. Its unique topography seems to have impressed George Bernard Shaw:

"The most fantastic and impossible rock in the world ... the thing does not belong to any world that you and I have lived and worked in; it is part of our dream world."

GEORGE BERNARD SHAW

I visited the island on a fairly sunny day in a sizeable boat. I was confused about why the skipper was handing out thick sou'westers on such a fine day. I got my answer once we left the harbour at Portmagee and entered the open seas. Rough doesn't do them justice. I'd hate to imagine what they'd be like on a bad day. The skipper told us we had a sixty–forty chance of docking and, by the time we reached the Sceilig, I was praying we would make it into the little pier. Either that or I would ask the skipper to throw me overboard and put me out of my misery. On the third approach, we docked and had a very pleasant sunny day on the island, until it was time to go home, of course!

Skellig Michael is a beautiful but barren and incredibly steep island. The climb to the top is arduous and tricky but hugely worthwhile when you finally arrive at the monastic settlement with its remnants of ancient church, monks' cells, high crosses, raised vegetable beds. I was in awe at the feat of construction involved in this community, and when I heard that the monks who first settled there in the sixth century to begin building this settlement had to row to the mainland to gather the stones, I was mesmerised. There was no flat stone on the island so they had to bring it all in, construct the steep pathway and then the numerous other buildings. You'd wonder why they chose such an austere and difficult location for their monastery. Maybe the answer lies in these lines from a ninth-century poem.

"I wish, O son of the Living God,
ancient eternal King, for a secret hut in the
wilderness, that it may be my dwelling."

I suppose this was their pilgrimage and their way of establishing a settlement in which their successors could also worship God in peace and solitude. I don't think it's possible for any of us to fully appreciate the physical effort and endurance of establishing a monastic settlement on Skellig Michael entailed. To say nothing of those constant trips forwards and backwards across that angry Atlantic sea! I didn't envy them but I did admire them. They deserve to be honoured in the same way as other people in other holy places have been honoured by pilgrims through the centuries. The fact that Skellig Michael is a UNESCO-designated World Heritage Site is a fitting tribute to the monks and their legacy.

I suppose I have a greater appreciation now of what Chaucer was on about in his *Canterbury Tales*. I hope Mr Fanagan would be pleased. Better late than never. I now share in the enthusiasm of pilgrimage, of walking the path and looking forward with anticipation and enthusiasm to what I learn as I walk. A bit like Sir Walter Raleigh in his poem 'The Passionate Man's Pilgrimage':

"Give me my scallop-shell of quiet,
My staff of faith to walk upon,
My script of joy, immortal diet,
My bottle of salvation,
My gown of glory, hopes true gage,
And thus I'll take my pilgrimage."

Sir Walter Raleigh

Mind, Body, Spirit

"Thou shalt respect the body as the highest manifestation of life.
Thou shalt nourish the body with only natural, unprocessed, 'live' food.
Thou shalt extend thy years in health for loving, charitable service.
Thou shalt keep thy thoughts, words and emotions pure, calm and uplifting.
Thou shalt regenerate thy body by the right balance of activity and rest."

Those are six of the ten 'Health Commandments', as published in a health magazine that advocated the benefits of apple cider vinegar for general well being. I came across them when I fulfilled a long-held ambition last spring. Towards the top of my wish list for quite a few years has been the desire to ... walk the Great Wall of China? Yes, someday. Visit the International Space Station? I'd love that, but it's unlikely. Nearer to home is a Health and Detox Centre just outside Westport in County Mayo and I realised my dream of spending time at such a place in March 2011. In the past, I've been pampered at delightful luxurious spa locations here in Ireland and abroad and loved every aspect of them – the massage with scented oils, the warm towels, the tranquil setting punctuated by soothing music and the sound of trickling water, all blending together to create an atmosphere of relaxation and general well being. Beethoven would have approved:

"Music is the mediator between
the spiritual and the sensual life."

LUDWIG VAN BEETHOVEN

I have also been vigorously massaged in less luxurious surroundings in parts of the developing world. A Thai masseuse walked, barefoot, up and down my back during my trip to Sri Lanka with GOAL in the wake of the tsunami. In Addis Ababa, during a Playing for Life trip to Ethiopia, strong African women with amazingly powerful hands and arms eased my aching limbs, eventually. I use the term 'eventually' for a good reason. There were times during those sessions when I thought I might be propelled head first through the wall of the massage parlour, such was the force of the action on my back. There were no frills attached, but once I recovered from the ordeal, my knotted, tense back was a whole lot looser. I realise the value of such encounters and fully agree with the stance of the World Health Organization:

"Health is a state of complete physical, mental and social well being, and not merely the absence of disease or infirmity."

WORLD HEALTH ORGANIZATION

I have been very lucky to have escaped disease and infirmity during my more than half century. The only times I was hospitalised were with appendicitis when I was twenty and then four times to give birth to my children. I realise that is a great gift and I don't take it for granted. There are many women, and men for that matter, of my age who do not enjoy 'rude good health' as they say. There are many people my age who seem older than their years. I accept that the ageing process brings with it certain challenges. But, as I said in an earlier chapter, I no longer fight against it. I'm enjoying this stage in life now, while accepting that I have to expend more effort to remain flexible and supple and active and I'm happy to put in that effort. I intend to enjoy life to the full for many years to come and I have to admit that although my body is ageing, I don't feel any older in my mind or spirit. I suppose two out of three ain't bad! James A. Garfield, President of the United States for a mere two hundred days in 1881 before he was assassinated, summed up my case as I see it:

"If wrinkles must be written upon our brow,
let them not be written upon the heart.
The spirit should not grow old."

James A. Garfield

I'm with President Garfield on that. There are ways of keeping the mind and spirit youthful while maximising the potential of the body at all stages of life, and my trip to a detox and health resort in March was something I had wanted to do for a long time. I wanted to eat healthy, unprocessed food without any possibility of giving in to my weakness for crusty bread. I wanted to think differently about what I ate, to concentrate on health and well being and set myself some new standards for the future care of body, mind and spirit. I feel privileged to be in good general health and am conscious that there are many who are not so privileged. There's a memorial stone near the pier in Cill Éinne on Inis Mór, the largest of the Aran Islands. It faces out to sea and it was erected to commemorate those who had lost their lives at sea. I took a photograph of its inscription when I was visiting my sister Deirdre on the island last year. It's on my fridge door along with the Ugandan photo about what money can't buy:

"Ní bhfaighidh siad sean mar a fhaigheann muide sean. Ní dhéanfaidh an tseanaois tinn agus craptha iad. Ná ní bhfaighidh na blianta locht orthu. Ach nuair a éiríonn an ghrian ar maidin agus nuair a théann sí faoi trathnóna, cuimhníonn muid orthu."

("They will not grow old as we grow old.
Old age will not make them ill and stooped.
The years will not find fault with them,
but when the sun rises in the morning and
when it sets in the evening, we remember them.")

What a sweet and sad thought. Young men lost at sea, their lives cut short in their prime. Life is a gift and living it well I think is a way of showing gratitude for that gift. To that end, I took myself out of circulation and headed to the health resort. 'Resort' is probably not the best word to use when describing the place. It may be misleading and in fairness to the centre it uses the word 'retreat'. That describes it well, I think. It is a retreat without the prayers, although yoga every morning can be a spiritual experience. As well as exercising, you're in tune with your inner self and your spirit:

"Yoga means union – the union of body with consciousness and consciousness with the soul."

B.K.S. Iyengar

Those are the words of B.K.S. Iyengar, one of the foremost yoga teachers in the world. He was born in 1918 into a poor family in India. He was sickly and weak during most of his childhood and fell victim to malaria, tuberculosis, typhoid fever and malnutrition at various stages. When he was fifteen, he lived with his brother-in-law, learned yoga and his health improved dramatically. He went on to achieve great fame as a yoga instructor. The good news is he's still with us and celebrates his ninety-second birthday in December. Hard to imagine, given his early medical history. A good advertisement for the practice certainly.

Yoga every morning was a highlight of the week. There's no doubt that worries and tensions were dispelled during those classes.

"Yoga has a sly, clever way of short-circuiting the mental patterns that cause anxiety."

Those are the words of a young American yoga master, and they reflect accurately how I felt during those sessions. I'm a person who always has some line of poetry or quotation rattling around in my head and the one that seemed to pop into my consciousness during those classes was from one of Shakespeare's sonnets:

"All losses are restored and sorrows end."

William Shakespeare

There are other ways in which the week felt like a retreat. The rooms were basic, some of them en suite, all with a single bed, a locker, a wardrobe and a chair. They were comfortable and warm. I smiled to myself as I unpacked my suitcase and found myself carefully hanging up my tracksuit bottoms and folding my T-shirts. There was going to be no need for heels or fancy clobber during this week. No need for television, radio, newspapers, mobile phones either, and no chance because they were on the banned list! Hard at first, but very liberating as well. Lots of time to walk in the beautiful countryside, to read and reflect and let's face it that was the purpose of the exercise.

There were also ways in which the week felt a bit like being in hospital. I and the five other women on the course had nothing to do all day but take part in inner cleansing procedures and present ourselves for meals at appointed times. No need for excitement now. We're talking very definite and very Spartan meals. Fresh fruit and vegetables, mostly raw. A shot of wheatgrass every morning got the day off to a healthy start. On the first day, it tasted fresh and green. By the end of the week, the yum had turned to yeuch. It lost its appeal to the palate but not to the system. Wheatgrass is acknowledged as one of the world's superfoods. I knocked it back as if it were a shot of something more sociable, like Tequila! There were tablespoons of cider vinegar to fit into the schedule also and at least three pints of warm water, all to be taken separately, with specific time lapses between the different elements. You see what I mean by it feeling akin to a hospital experience. Nurse Ratched from *One Flew Over The Cuckoo's Nest* was there in spirit with a reminder when it was 'medication time'.

The only cooked item was vegetable soup at lunch-time. And how we looked forward to that. The fact that it was beautifully presented along with two appetising and interesting salads added to its appeal. We're talking spinach and coconut soup accompanied by guacamole in salad form and another salad of perhaps grated carrot, parsnip and ginger topped with a sesame oil and cider-vinegar dressing. It sounds delicious on paper and believe me, when you've had nothing but one grapefruit and two oranges for breakfast six hours previously, it not only sounded delicious, it tasted delicious as well! Lunch was the main meal of the day and also its culinary highlight. It was followed by a walk in the uplifting surroundings with views over Clew Bay and Croagh Patrick. This walk was contrary to what my body thought it wanted. Following a meal, I'm inclined to relax with a cuppa (poison if it's got a whiff of caffeine), but, to be honest, the one-and-a-half-hour walk did wonders for the digestion of the 'main meal'.

The walks were delightful. We were blessed with good weather, the scenery was stunning and it was springtime so we were walking through areas bedecked with daffodils and looking at tiny lambs, new to the world, all white and fluffy.

The scene reminded me of a poem I love by Katharine Tynan, a poet and novelist for whom I have particular affection because she was born, in 1861, in my home village of Clondalkin. She was from a farming background and ended up being friendly with the likes of Yeats (rumour has it he proposed to her, but she said no). She was also friendly with Gerard Manley Hopkins and Francis Ledwidge. Katharine married a barrister, wrote more than a hundred novels and died in England in 1931. I'm very proud of the fact that she came from the same place as I did, and I cannot for the life of me understand why Katharine Tynan was not fêted and talked about in my school. It's only now I realise the significance of the landmark we used as youngsters for our blackberry-picking escapades. We always vowed we'd keep picking till we got to Tynan's Cross. We had no notion that this spot marked the home place of a woman of substance, worthy of recognition and veneration as an accomplished, thoughtful Irish woman. What does that say about us as a race of people? Her words that I thought about as I went on those after-lunch walks during that week of health and well being in the west of Ireland are:

"All in the April morning,
April airs were abroad;
The sheep with their little lambs
Pass'd me by on the road."

KATHARINE TYNAN

As well as being a woman ahead of her time in terms of literature and poetry, she was also a woman of great faith. The poem relates the story of the lamb to that of Jesus, the Lamb of God:

"All in the April evening.
April airs were abroad;
I saw the sheep with their lambs,
And thought of the Lamb of God."

KATHARINE TYNAN

Our last meal of the day was at six o'clock. If I were to ask my stomach which of the three meals of the day it looked forward to least, it would undoubtedly be the tae! Arranged on a very nice navy-blue Westport pottery plate was a banana, a kiwi, grapes, an apple and some dried fruit. Accompanied by a few provisos. All with good reason, I may add. But nonetheless a pain in the neck! You don't drink while you're eating. Just to clarify, we're talking water here. But, no. Not good to eat and drink at the same time. There's no chance of a slice of bread or a wedge of cheese to add a bit of variety either. It's a detox after all. I did manage to elicit a few laughs from the group when I sat down at the bench on the second evening and suggested that the banana could look like a skinny striploin. We survived though. I never felt hungry. In fact there were times when I felt quite full, but I accept that was because of the change of diet. No bread, nothing processed at all, just good, healthy – mostly raw – food.

I said earlier that the morning yoga sessions were a highlight. The other highlight happened in the evening after our sumptuous tea! It was sauna followed by massage followed by bed. Pure bliss! Or so it would seem. The sauna was delightful but we were under detox instructions which ordained that we spend ten minutes in the sauna before subjecting ourselves to an icy cold shower and then a repeat of the process before meriting the luxurious relaxing pre-sleep massage. And that massage was lovely, sleep inducing, but I feel it important to outline how horrific and awful was the cold shower that punctuated our sauna sessions. I just couldn't hack it. I noticed that the shower rose was detachable, and having released it from its position I used it, hand held to tease my body with fleeting sprays of ice cold water until the time was up and the water ceased to flow. That couldn't have happened soon enough. The brave souls in our group who stood in under the shower and endured the torture provided us with no end of entertainment while we listened to their gasps of pain and horror. Those gasps gave way to sighs of relaxation as we lined up for massage before bedtime. Hippocrates, the ancient Greek physician, said of massage therapy way back in the fourth century BC:

"The physician must be experienced in
many things, but most assuredly in rubbing.
For rubbing can bind a joint that is loose,
and loosen a joint that is too rigid."

HIPPOCRATES

More than two thousand years later, massage is still an essential part of well being and the massage therapists in

Mayo were certainly experienced in rubbing. They worked wonders on the tired bodies of us detoxers as we prepared to sleep off the adventure of that day's experience.

All in all, that detox and health week was an important one for me. It changed the way I think about food and the way I think about my body. I will be paying a return visit there for sure. I learned that it takes a half hour for your body to digest fruit and an hour and a half for vegetables, whereas it takes up to eight hours to digest animal foodstuffs. Seems like a no brainer really, that it's important to eat a lot more of the fruit and veg than we do. It was a no brainer in the seventeenth century, when François de la Rochefoucauld was writing maxims, and the wisdom hasn't changed since then:

"To eat is a necessity, but to eat intelligently is an art."

FRANÇOIS DE LA ROCHEFOUCAULD

For me, to eat intelligently means consuming the greens and the raw foods in much larger quantities than I was used to. I'm the classic weak-willed eater, who is a paragon of virtue when I'm full and my appetite is satisfied. When I'm hungry though, or even just peckish, I start doing deals with myself, trading off a bit of instant gratification in the form of crusty fresh bread and butter with a vow to just have soup and vegetables the following day. That vow generally ends up on the cutting room floor, as they say in movie land. I think the American columnist Doug Larson had me in mind when he spoke about food:

"Life expectancy would grow by leaps and bounds
If green vegetables tasted as good as bacon."

DOUG LARSON

I was quite surprised by the effects on my system of the detox, which required that I cut out all caffeine, tea, even green tea, coffee, Coke, alcohol, red meat and sugary foods for a week before even hitting the health resort. My friends were mesmerised that I was using up a week of my precious annual leave to go to this place, where, in their opinion, I would be starving. To spend the week beforehand enduring the effects of the toxins leaving the body convinced them I had lost the plot altogether! The lack of caffeine had dramatic effects. These started with piercing headaches which lasted for a day. That evening, I could barely keep my eyes open past dinner time. Those reminders that my body wanted its caffeine fix paled into insignificance compared to the following day's onslaught, which saw me writhing in pain from my back down to my ankles. The British television personality Carol Vorderman has written books about detoxing and is an advocate of the practice:

"The first couple of days on
the detox diet aren't pleasant."

CAROL VORDERMAN

Having endured the pains in my legs as they cried out for their usual coating of toxins, I would say that Carol is a master of understatement. I never experienced anything like it before and I was genuinely frightened that there was something seriously wrong with me. There was, I suppose. My lifestyle was one of drinking tea all day. The first thing I did when I came down to the kitchen in the morning was to fill the kettle. I looked forward to my coffee mid-morning and tea right through the rest of the day. I looked forward to the last cup of tea in bed before I fell asleep. Awful I know, but it could be worse. My father looked forward to his last cigarette of the day in bed before he fell asleep! I'm delighted to report that I didn't go back to my nasty habits with regard to constant tea and coffee drinking, often at the expense of proper meals. Who was I kidding?

For far too many years, in my mind, food and body were deadly enemies. I wanted the perfect body. Food was the enemy. The problem lay in the fact that I actually like food and, as I get older, I appreciate the fact that food is not only fuel for the body but also very much part of social interaction and convivial living. It delights me also to realise and acknowledge that my adult children appreciate food in a way that just didn't exist when I was their age. Eva and Tom, my two older children, spent a Thursday evening recently at a three-hour Spanish cookery course. What a pleasant way to spend an evening. Not a chance of that happening when I was their age. When I was growing up, it was all about being skinny minnies, wanting to emulate the Mary Quant models and Twiggy. The fact that they were the exception to our norm didn't seem to register with us and led to an awful lot of angst as I and my pals aspired but failed to live up to those role models. When I

think back to those days now, all I can think of saying is, 'What a load of rubbish.' But try telling that to me and my pals way back then!

For me now, the important thing is to be healthy and to maximise the possibilities for well being into the next stage of my life. This is a new way of thinking, believe me. I hope there are people reading this who will say to themselves, 'Do you know what? I've been thinking that way as well.' What a liberation when that moment hit me on the head and, more importantly, in the heart. I wish I hadn't spent so many years striving for bodily perfection, a striving that was, at best, skewed, at worst, irrational, impossible, undesirable even. Now that I've made peace with the stupidity of those wasted years of striving for nothingness, the words of the nineteenth-century American preacher William Ellery Channing strike a particularly relevant chord:

> *"... to seek elegance rather than luxury,*
> *and refinement rather than fashion;*
> *to be worthy, not respectable,*
> *and wealthy, not rich."*
>
> William Ellery Channing

Those are far more worthy aspirations, and far more likely to bring success and happiness in their pursuit than the preoccupations of my mind as I was growing up. I have finally laid that ghost to rest and I thank this middle stage of life for giving me that insight into the beauty and value of life. And it's a million miles away from size zero! It's unfortunate that we get so caught up with appearances and symbols of status and wealth. I have come to a stage in life where I have scant regard for the trappings and where the essence of the interaction I can have with people and circumstances is what works for me. The most important aspect of all of that though is the total letting go of any aspirations to be like the people who still hold the style and material aspects of life and living to be of great importance. I acknowledge their interest and commitment to that fluctuating element of life, but I don't envy them or want to be there again with them. Last summer, I came across a magazine interview with the wonderfully stylish and talented French model Inés de la Fressange. This year, at the age of fifty-one, she modelled in the Chanel Spring–Summer Show, having previously been the muse of Karl Lagerfeld. In *Paris Match,* she was asked for her definition of elegance:

"Elle est le reflet de votre esprit et n'a rien a voir avec le vêtement. Un clochard peut-être elegant, mais une femme qui a des pensées vulgaires ne le sera pas."

("It is the reflection of your spirit and has nothing to do with clothes. A tramp can be elegant but a woman who has vulgar thoughts will never be elegant.")

INÉS DE LA FRESSANGE

❧

Nice to think that this physically beautiful woman realises that it's not just about the exterior. She must have fought the good fight to get that thinking on board in the world she frequented when she was modelling on the most stylish catwalks in the world. I find it very encouraging to hear words like that from a woman of such standing. Another stunningly beautiful woman who, like Inés, kept a head on her shoulders and didn't 'lose the run of herself' was Audrey Hepburn, who liked to remind people in the world of stardom and beauty and all that went with it:

❧

"For attractive lips, speak words of kindness.
For lovely eyes, seek out the good in people."

AUDREY HEPBURN

You'd walk a long way before you'd come upon such a sensible and down to earth outlook in the world of film and fashion today, methinks.

Reflecting back to those ten health commandments, it really does come down to a sense of balance. I wasted far too many years striving for what I thought of as perfection. What was it only skinniness, artificiality and lots more besides. I am now at a stage in life where I realise that I have probably lived longer than I will live into the future. I have striven for the unattainable for too long and I have now decided that I will live and make the most of every minute of every day I spend on this earth:

"To awaken each morning with a smile
brightening my face; to greet the day
with reverence for the opportunities it contains."

THOMAS DEKKER

That's my new aspiration. I find it fascinating that those lines, written by Thomas Dekker, an Elizabethan poet and playwright who died in 1641, still have such relevance nearly four hundred years later. Some things never change; the good things never change. The piece finishes with another few lines that have become one of my mantras:

"To approach the night
with weariness that ever woos sleep and the joy
that comes from work well done –
this is how I desire to waste wisely my days."

Is there anything nicer than falling into bed, physically tired after a productive day, and embarking on the second phase of regenerating the body 'by the right balance of activity and rest'? Before I go to sleep, without that last cup of tea on my bedside locker, I like to go through a mental list of the good things that happened during the day. Hopefully, they include a mixture of work and play, of conversation and reflection. I try very hard to get that balance right. It's far too easy, at the end of a busy and demanding day, to just sit around and do nothing. I find that taking exercise or doing a bit of gardening or going out to socialise takes a lot of effort in the beginning, but I have never pushed myself to do any of those things and been sorry afterwards. I have often been sorry and annoyed with myself if I have given in to my tired and lazy self and turned down any opportunity.

There's an interesting book by the Japanese writer Haruki Murakami, the man who wrote *Norwegian Wood*. It's called *What I Talk About When I Talk About Running*. The title caught my imagination. Not surprising, because until my knees told me to hang up my running shoes, I enjoyed running so much. The book outlines Murakami's physical and psychological approach to taking up long-distance running. He only got bitten by the bug in his thirties when he sold his jazz bar to devote his life to writing. He took up running at the same time to keep fit. He has some interesting observations to make about living life and the analogies he makes with preparing for a marathon, for instance. On the subject of hitting a good balance in life between work and play, he has this to say:

"I'm struck by how, except when you're young, you really have to prioritise in life, figuring out in what order you should divide up your time

and energy. If you don't get that sort of system set by a certain age, you'll lack focus and your life will be out of balance."

Haruki Murakami

ᘓ

Good advice that. A reminder that energy can be redirected and regenerated even when I'm tired and the result will be a nice mix of work and leisure activity to be grateful for as I lie in bed awaiting sleep at the end of a fulfilling day. I enjoyed reading Murakami's book because I really enjoyed the many years I spent running. I miss it hugely. I still exercise with Pilates and walking but it's not the same. There's something about running that pushes you a little bit further than your comfort zone and that is a very satisfying feeling when you finish a run, exhausted but uplifted. As Murakami says:

ᘓ

"Most runners run because they want to live life to the fullest. If you're going to while away the years, it's far better to live them with clear goals and fully alive than in a fog, and I believe running helps you to do that."

Haruki Murakami

ꝛ

Well said. Who wants to live life in a fog? Not me. I want to have clear goals and energy to fulfil them, and I honestly believe I have, at long last, reached a point in life where I acknowledge that the way I treat my body and the food I put into it has a central part to play in being fog free and full of beans.

Hanging on the kitchen wall in the health and detox centre, authored by Swami Satyananda Saraswati, was a Declaration of Freedom. Swami Satyananda, who died in 2009 at the age of eighty-six, was highly revered in his native India and all around the world as a yoga master and guru. He founded the International Yoga Federation in 1956. Swami had heightened spiritual experiences from the age of six and lived the life of a monk in various ashrams. His declaration of freedom struck a chord with me as I progressed during the week of detox, so I took a photo of it on my phone just before I left, to have it when I got home. It sums up the value I got from taking a step outside of my comfort zone and going, on my own, to this health and detox centre. I had never gone away on my own before.

The sojourn was an opportunity to reassess who I am and where I am and I'm pleased that I made changes to my lifestyle that have been beneficial. It goes to show that it's never too late to learn, it's never too late to change, it's never too late to be free:

"Instead of wishing that you were free to live your life differently, accept the truth that right now you are free ... Free to change your thinking, free to change your outlook on life, free to be all that you long to be."

SWAMI SATYANANDA SARASWATI

Comfort on Difficult Days

"The ideals which have lighted my way,
and time after time have given me new courage
to face life cheerfully, have been kindness,
beauty, and truth."

ALBERT EINSTEIN

These words of Albert Einstein took on an extra resonance with me the week before I finished writing this book. I was so looking forward to starting the final chapter. I was proud of what I had achieved, on target to have the whole thing completed by the appointed date. I had put a lot of work into the research and the writing in my spare time since the start of the year. I had come to terms with the fact that you can't make an omelette without breaking eggs and that I can't write a book without having the house looking a bit neglected, not to mention the garden that I was dying to get my hands on when, after the awful winter, I realised that:

"Spring is sprung, the grass is riz."

I resisted the temptation however to tackle the very sad and forlorn-looking house and garden and spent all my free time at the paper-strewn dining-room table. I had been diligent and focused, and now the end was in sight. I just wanted to gather all of my thoughts together and finish off on a positive note. I was pleased I had accepted the publisher's invitation to put some more musings and sayings together. I admit I was ambivalent at the beginning, unsure whether I could cope with the extra workload and shy about the prospect of talking about this middle stage of life. However, I bit that bullet and because I am now content with where I am in life, agreed to actually write about it. I am firmly of the opinion expressed by William James when he wrote:

"How pleasant is the day when we give up striving to be young ... or slender."

William James

ꝸ

William James is an interesting man. A doctor and also one of the most prominent American psychologists and philosophers of the nineteenth century, William was the brother of the novelist Henry James and their sister was the diarist Alice James. I think you could describe them as a family of high achievers! His godfather was another great American thinker, the essayist and poet Ralph Waldo Emerson. I came across William James in a book about Emerson, a writer who fascinates me always for the fact that he describes exactly how I'm thinking and feeling, despite the fact that he died one hundred and thirty years ago! His insight into the human condition, and for this fan, the female condition, is deep and inspirational:

ꝸ

"Be not the slave of your own past.
Plunge into the sublime seas,
dive deep and swim far,
so you shall come back with self-respect,
with new power,
with an advanced experience
that shall explain and overlook the old."

Ralph Waldo Emerson

❦

Wouldn't that just make you want to get up off that couch and take the plunge into new adventures and experiences? I'll return to the slouch on the couch syndrome in a little while! Emerson also has a lovely view of ageing:

❦

"As we grow old ... the beauty steals inward."

RALPH WALDO EMERSON

❦

Perhaps Emerson's particular understanding of women is due in some degree to the fact that his father died of cancer just two weeks before his eighth birthday and Ralph was reared by his mother and other women in the family, notably his aunt, Mary Moody, who lived with them and to whom he was particularly close. This interest in and insight into the human condition with all its joys and sorrows seems to have rubbed off on his godson, William James, who is renowned for defining true beliefs as those that prove useful to the believer. I can't see anything wrong with that:

ↄ

"Be not afraid of life. Believe that life is worth living, and your belief will help create the fact."

William James

ↄ

So, with the words of Emerson and James ringing in my ears, I embarked on what has been an exhausting but satisfying time of writing some lines that I find useful for living, lines that give me hope sometimes, or comfort, or a cattle prod in the back to do something different. Having written eleven chapters, all with different themes, and having patted myself on the back, I was really looking forward to writing the final chapter in the hope that when readers would put this book down, they too would feel motivated or comforted by the words that have that effect on me.

Then my confidence took a bit of a battering. It happened very simply. I was in the house alone around five o'clock in the evening and answered a knock at the door to be greeted by a tall, well-built man who handed me his flyer and asked if I'd like my chimney swept. His van was parked outside with his company details printed on the side. The chimneys were in real need of a

good clean so, after a bit of haggling, we agreed a price and two other men came in and proceeded to do the job. They then suggested that I should have cowls on the chimney pots to deter birds from nesting. While fitting them, one of the workers realised the chimney was loose and needed a bit of cement. When this job was done, there was some cement left over and he said he'd fill in the gaps at the edge of the slates. He told me there were some missing and broken slates and he'd replace them. Are you getting the picture?

All the while this work was proceeding, I was there with the men. I did what I always do when people are working in my house, I made them tea and chatted with them while they worked. That kindness that Einstein referred to in the lines at the beginning of this chapter is the correct way to behave towards others as far as I'm concerned. In this instance, it was definitely a mistake. All the time they were drinking that tea and talking, they were thinking up other 'little jobs' that they'd do for me while they were here. I took them at their word. Truth is another of Einstein's ideals above. My jaw dropped when they told me how much I owed them. I thought they were joking. But they weren't. Slowly, it began to dawn on me that I had been had. In the heel of the hunt, I paid an exorbitant amount of money for bitty little jobs. I was afraid not to. They knew I was alone in the house. I was a little bit unnerved and just wanted rid of them. I also felt this was a minor, though expensive, upheaval in my life compared to what other people endure. I felt very, very stupid. How often have I listened to people on *Liveline* telling their tales of woe about fraudsters and wondered how anyone can be so stupid to be taken in by these people? Now I know. I am that soldier. I was pretty shaken by the episode. For a start, I handed out far too much money for nothing. I was angry, frustrated and a bit frightened by the experience. What if they came back, realising that I was such a soft touch? I hated the fact that they had lied at every turn to me, that they conned me totally. This was my *Liveline* moment! An American lawyer called Charles Simmons has written of fraud:

"For the most part fraud in the end secures for its companions repentance and shame."

Charles Simmons

I think the only person who experienced repentance and shame in this instance was me. I was so sorry I had opened the door that evening and I was ashamed that I was so naïve as to be taken in by those men. In my defence, though, they were experienced and clever at their craft. Steven Spielberg couldn't have written a better script! They were believable and utterly shameless. I do not think repentance and shame will strike them any time soon.

It was an unpleasant experience and a lesson learned. I'm over it now. It was, however, the start of a trying week. My car broke down. Our very old and much-loved dog showed signs of decline and spent two nights in the dog hospital. There's another section to that piece by Albert Einstein, though, that I also remind myself of when life is trying:

"The trite subjects of human efforts –
possessions, outward success, luxury –
have always seemed to me contemptible."

Albert Einstein

A bit strong perhaps, but a reminder nonetheless that, for happiness and fulfilment in life, material trappings are not going to be much help. It's important to make the best of situations. The car has been fixed. The dog has rallied a little bit and is home with the people who love him to bits. And my chimneys are cleaned and fitted with galvanised cowls. There will be no birds' nests there from now on. Mind you, there were no birds' nests there before last week either, but let's not go there!

As well as making the best of situations, it's also important to make the most of opportunities. I am convinced that effort breeds energy. I am often reluctant to get up from the couch and go to do something, but I know that if I give into that reluctance, I will be visited by a dose of regret and self-disgust later on. On the other hand, if I make the effort, I will not only be glad afterwards, but my energies will be restored. 'Just do it' is quite a good maxim to keep in mind. Life is short. Life is precious. We should live every moment fully. I'm a great fan of the American poet Maya Angelou and she often refers to the beauty of life and the need to live it now. In her poem 'When Great Trees Fall', she talks about what happens after death, and these lines always reverberate with me:

"When great souls die …
Our memory, suddenly sharpened,
examines,
gnaws on kind words
unsaid,
promised walks
never taken."

MAYA ANGELOU

What a shame for that to happen. No point in holding back. Life is for living, people are for loving. Therefore, no matter how tired I am, I remember those words of Maya Angelou and Ralph Waldo Emerson and I will get up off that couch and go for that walk. I will plunge into 'the sublime seas' and come back with a little bit more self-respect than when I left.

As for the 'kind words unsaid' that Angelou refers to, I made a resolution some years ago to overcome my shyness and say nice things to people. They really can give a soul a lift and a feeling of well being. Mother Teresa put it well when she said:

"Kind words can be short and easy to speak, but their echoes are truly endless."

Mother Teresa

ঌ

I have an inner smile in my heart when someone says something positive to me, so I reckon it's the same for others as well. There's a nice moment in *Eat, Pray, Love*, the book written by Elizabeth Gilbert about the year she spent travelling and gaining different experiences after the breakup of her marriage. From time to time, Elizabeth battled with negative thoughts. A friend says to her:

ঌ

"You need to be able to select your thoughts just the same way you select what clothes you're gonna wear each day."

Elizabeth Gilbert

ঌ

Good advice there, and, having received it, Elizabeth devised a personal vow that she repeated to herself each day:

"I will not harbour unhealthy thoughts anymore."

ELIZABETH GILBERT

Easier said than done, of course, but well worth the effort, because not only do other people benefit from my positive thoughts, I do too. Mind you, my positive thoughts about the workmen who entered my life last week didn't do me any good. Or did they?

"Whenever evil befalls us, we ought to ask ourselves, after the first suffering, how we can turn it into good. So shall we take occasion, from one bitter root, to raise many flowers."

LEIGH HUNT

Those are the words of the English publisher and poet Leigh Hunt, the man who introduced Keats to Shelley and moved in the same circles as other literary luminaries of nineteenth-century England, such as Lord Byron.

Hunt had a difficult life all in all. He and his wife suffered long periods of ill health and he was constantly in financial trouble. Evil things certainly befell him and it's nice to think that he looked on the bright side and raised 'many flowers' from his experiences.

But what flowers can I raise from my roofing escapade? I have certainly learned a valuable lesson. I have told my story to family and friends and, although sympathetic, they could see a funny side that seems to have eluded me. I know I handed over good money for nothing but, to be honest, I would rather be me in that situation than them. I would hate to be so unfeeling about other people. I'm lucky this was a one-off experience. I know there are people who have had much worse experiences than mine, and I feel for them. I hope they have love and support to help them cope, to move on and to enjoy this beautiful life.

I can't think of any better way of drawing this chapter and this book to a close than with these lines from A.A. Milne's delightful children's story *Winnie the Pooh*, which I read to all of my children when they were very small. These lines had a resonance for me the very first time I read them and that resonance has intensified as I have journeyed through different stages of motherhood from reading bedtime stories to correcting homework and being a chauffeur, to having four adult children that provide meaning and purpose in my life. This is what I wish for them as they take their place in the adult world and as I watch them and root for them from this glorious and satisfying middle stage of life:

"This is my wish for you:
Comfort on difficult days,
smiles when sadness intrudes,
rainbows to follow the clouds,
laughter to kiss your lips,
sunsets to warm your heart,
hugs when spirits sag,
beauty for your eyes to see,
friendships to brighten your being,
faith so that you can believe,
confidence for when you doubt,
courage to know yourself,
patience to accept the truth,
Love to complete your life."

A.A. Milne